First published in the UK by Michael Joseph, an imprint of Penguin Books Ltd.

HarperCollins books may be purchased for educational, business, or sales promotional use. For information please write: Special Markets Department, HarperCollins Publishers, 10 East 53rd Street, New York, NY 10022.

FIRST U.S. EDITION

Library of Congress Cataloging-in-Publication Data has been applied for.

ISBN 978-0-06-204972-8

11   12   13   14   15   Dix/Penguin UK   10   9   8   7   6   5   4   3   2   1

AT ELIZABETH DAVID'S TABLE

CLASSIC RECIPES *and* TIMELESS KITCHEN WISDOM

Elizabeth David

Compiled and with an Introduction by Jill Norman

Preface by Ruth Reichl

Photography by David Loftus

Illustrations by Jon Gray

ecco

An Imprint of HarperCollinsPublishers

CONTENTS

PREFACE

"Always do as you please, and send everybody to Hell, and take the consequences. Damned good Rule of Life." When Elizabeth David was in her twenties, Norman Douglas wrote that in her copy of *Old Calabria*. She spent the rest of her life following his advice.

It is that—more than her vividly evocative writing or seductively simple recipes—that made me fall in love with Elizabeth David the first time that we met. I was sixteen, and our encounter was strictly literary. Browsing the magazines in a thrift shop, I was thumbing through an old issue of English *Vogue* when I came upon one of her articles. It was a shock.

At the time most of the people writing about food were good girls—motherly creatures who stood by the stove ladling out sage advice. Elizabeth David, on the other hand, was a wild woman. "I think we must both have been more than a little tipsy," she said of the moment Douglas told her to please only herself. No surprise there. Betty Crocker might have considered a glass of warm milk a suitable nightcap; Elizabeth David most definitely did not.

I was a lonely girl who loved to cook, stuck in an America that considered hamburgers the epitome of fine food, and I was very fortunate to have found Elizabeth David. She was everything I was not: unconventional, sensuous, smart and stylish. She was a woman who loved men (and was loved by them), and cared not one whit about anyone's opinion of her. I instantly knew that I wanted to be just like her.

That was going to take time. I had never tasted the kind of food she was writing about, but when she described a lakeside picnic in the south of France (music provided by a convenient waterfall), it seemed like a promise that the experience was out there, waiting for me. "As you drink wine from a tumbler, sprinkle your bread with olive oil and salt, and eat it with ripe tomatoes or rough country sausage you feel better off than in even the most perfect restaurant," she wrote. I sat in my room, reading that, knowing that I would one day fly off to France and find my waterfall.

Her description of eating white truffles was much more satisfying than the rhapsodic accounts of other writers, who ate them served over pasta or scrambled into eggs. I'd never tasted truffles, but I knew I wanted to do it à la Elizabeth (by now we were on a first-name basis). "We drank a bottle of red Dolcetto, a local wine and a dry and genuine one, and then some bread and butter spread with truffles. (This is one of the best ways of eating them if you can ever persuade a Piedmontese to allow you such a simple treat.)" Sure enough, when I finally went to Italy and ate truffles, I had them on buttered bread. I highly recommend it.

But she was never content with simply romanticizing the experience of food. Other people could do that too. What made Elizabeth David stand out was how delightfully nasty she could be when provoked. In one of my favorite pieces, "*Exigez le veritable Cheddar français,*" she wrote about the German imposter which passed for Gruyère in England: "This is a cheese which is expensive, smells of drains—it is marketed in wrapped wedges so you do not find this out until you get it home—and in consistence is more suitable for mending tires than for the cooking pot. (One longs for the Germans to give up trying to make facsimiles of other people's cheeses. They are terrible duffers at it.)" By the time I read that I was considering food writing as a possible career, and this was extremely instructive. Apparently it was okay—no, imperative—to get angry at bad food. And more important, Elizabeth taught me that, in the recipe for food writing, humor is an essential ingredient.

Her own humor was always wry, and she had few illusions. When she collected recipes from the Mediterranean, she knew exactly what would happen once they made their way to British shores. Writing about the Catalan peasant's breakfast of garlic-rubbed bread (*pa y all*), she envisioned its fate in England. "It would become chopped garlic on toast made from factory bread, spread with salad cream and crowned with a pimento-stuffed olive (that is the Catalan part, we should be told). In time, a very short time probably, this creation would find its way into the nation's deep-freeze. There would be a curry version and a cheese variation and a super gigantic one with bacon, lettuce, onion rings and radishes." What this taught me was that recipes—no matter how good—were not enough. To really appreciate the food of another country, I was going to have to travel. I understood that for Elizabeth food transcended taste: it was also about the sounds, the smells, the markets. She started writing in chilly postwar England, hoping "to stir the memories of those who have eaten this food on its native shores, and who would like sometimes to bring a flavor of those blessed lands of sun and sea and olive trees into their English kitchens." Cooking was the next best thing to being there, but her feet were always restless and her bags were always packed.

But to truly understand Elizabeth David's legacy, you have to go beyond food and move into the kitchen. In the apartment I grew up in, cooking was considered a kind of shameful secret, and it was done in a walled-off room. When company came, dinner was supposed to magically appear, borne in on trays, as if it had been prepared in some faraway facility. Cooking odors were meant to know their place, which was behind the firmly closed kitchen door. Even good cooks practiced their art in private. Julia Child famously told her American audience, "Remember, you are alone in the kitchen and nobody can see you."

Elizabeth David was having none of that; she threw open the kitchen door and asked everyone in. "Some sensible person," she wrote, "once remarked that you spend the whole of your life either in your bed or your shoes. Having done the best you can by shoes and bed, devote all the time and resources at your disposal to the building up of a fine kitchen. It will be, as it should be, the most comforting and comfortable room in the house." The kitchen was the heart of her home; it was where she did her writing, surrounded by pots, pans, plates and herbs. Nothing was hidden, it was a kind of wonderful jumble of a mess with dishes tumbling out of open drawers. When friends showed up, she simply pushed her papers aside and invited them to join her at the table. She was rarely alone in the kitchen, and since she was fond of cats I've always imagined them in there too, nosing along the counters, leaping from surface to surface, investigating the good scents emerging from great copper pots. Her way was casual, and it sounded like much more fun than the grim, lonely science of the solitary cooks with whom I was familiar.

That is, ultimately, the difference between Elizabeth David and the other recipe writers of her time; she believed that cooking was fun, and she trusted you to find your own way of doing it. Her recipes were suggestions, not prescriptions; you were meant to cook something a little more or a little less, to use different herbs, throw in a bit of leftover wine. She didn't give you precise directions because she trusted you to taste as you cooked, to use both your mouth and your mind. She did as she pleased—and she expected you to do the same. Her recipes are starting points, and they are meant to seduce you into the kitchen; should you discover, once you get there, that you are lacking a few major ingredients, she expects that you will improvise. As a young cook, faced with the military precision of American cookbooks, I found her easygoing recipes were very liberating. I am incapable of following a recipe to the letter, and until I met Elizabeth I had always considered this to be a failing.

By the time I was in college I was pouncing on anything written by Elizabeth David, and when I saw that a 1970 issue of *Gourmet* had an article of hers, I immediately went out and got it. That was how I discovered my other favorite cookbook writer, Edouard de Pomiane. She was extolling *Cooking with Pomiane*, a collection of his letters, lectures and recipes, which was, she said, "still relatively unknown, modest in appearance and in size." Its jacket, she said, was "the reverse of eye-catching, there are no color photographs, no packaging. It is just a very good and immensely sane book." "Sane" is a high compliment from Elizabeth David and I ran right out and bought a copy.

Although Elizabeth was generous in her praise of the people that she loved, she could be brutal to those that she did not. She never pulled her punches. But even her nastiest published pieces seem like the height of politeness compared to the private thoughts she scrawled for her own edification. Reading through the notes in her own cookbooks (which were bequeathed to the London Guildhall library) is to get a glimpse of how utterly uncompromising this woman could be. Inside a copy of *The Food of Italy*, a classic book that most people discuss in reverent tones, she wrote, "Waverley Root is a pitiful phoney." (I loved reading that, because I've always suspected that he made half of his information up.) I bought *Ma Gastronomie* by the great Fernand Point after reading that Thomas Keller considered it an essential addition to a cook's library. I should have consulted Elizabeth first. "This," she wrote to herself, "is a really awful book."

In the late seventies I was treated to my very own taste of Elizabeth's scorn. Knowing that I was a devoted acolyte, a San Francisco friend invited me to a dinner he was planning for her at his Nob Hill home. I was both elated and terrified. I wanted, of course, to meet her, but I was afraid that she would turn out to be just another sweet little old lady. I need not have worried. She was in her seventies at the time, still stylish and still incapable of suffering fools. When I said something saccharine about how much I admired her work she gave me an acid smile and pointedly turned away. There were only a few of us at the table, but she made such cutting remarks that our host called later to apologize. Elizabeth, he said, could be difficult. Especially when she was on this side of the pond.

I didn't mind; the truth is that I was so dazzled by meeting her that I had been oblivious to her comments. If she had turned out to be politely ordinary, I would have been terribly disappointed, and I could certainly understand how difficult it must have been for her in America. At that point in her life she was an icon in England, universally acknowledged as "the most important cookery writer of the twentieth century." She was known as the woman who changed the way the English eat. Over there she was James Beard, Julia Child, MFK Fisher and Chuck Williams (she had a cookware shop for almost ten years) rolled into one. But most Americans had no idea who she was, and Elizabeth David was not the person to appreciate that.

Among food people she has always had a cult following, and every ten years or so another American version of an Elizabeth David book is printed. Each of them has an introduction by someone who is certain that she is finally about to get the recognition she deserves. "While it has taken some time," James Beard wrote in 1980, "I feel we in America are now ready for Elizabeth David. We have come of age in the culinary sense and acquired the skills and confidence to accept her on her own terms."

It seems he was wrong, because some twenty years later, Molly O'Neill was, once again, trying to convince us of the importance of Elizabeth David. In the introduction to *Summer Cooking*, O'Neill noted that even though the recipes were almost half a century old, they were neither dated nor dowdy. The recipes, she wrote, were alive, and she had high hopes that they would help contemporary readers find their own voices in the kitchen.

Now another ten years have passed, and a generation that adores Jamie Oliver and Nigella Lawson still knows nothing about the woman who paved their way. I hope that this comprehensive book, the first to give these recipes the lush photographs they cry out for, will change that. There's never been anyone like Elizabeth David, and there undoubtedly never will be. She has so much more to tell us than merely how to cook. Her recipes are simple, sensuous and intuitive. They combine taste, texture and color. But reading between the lines you come to understand that what Elizabeth David is really saying is to savor every minute of your life.

She certainly did. Alive to every sense, she was a woman who refused to accept the possibility of eating badly. Faced with postwar privation she began to write—"out of an agonized craving for the sun and a furious revolt against the terrible, cheerless, heartless food. . . . Even to write words like apricot, olives and butter, rice and lemons, oil and almonds, produced assuagement." To Elizabeth David cooking was an affirmation of everything good about being alive, and reading her book makes you want to run right into the kitchen and become part of the generous, joyous, world in which she lived.

Ruth Reichl

INTRODUCTION

Elizabeth David was born in 1913, one of four daughters of Rupert and Stella Gwynne. Her father was Conservative MP for Eastbourne and she had a conventional middle-class upbringing, with nanny and governess. She later went to a girls' school where the food was decidedly inferior—"nothing will surely ever taste so hateful as nursery tapioca, or the appalling boiled cod of schooldays." At sixteen, she was sent to live with a French family in Passy, and if her studies at the Sorbonne did not leave a lasting impression, "what stuck was the taste for a kind of food quite ideally unlike anything I had known before." On her return to England she had a spell at the Oxford repertory theater and a brief acting career at the Open Air Theatre in Regent's Park.

In the late 1930s she went off with a lover to France, where she met the writer Norman Douglas—the two became firm friends in spite of the disparity in their ages (she was twenty-four and he seventy-two), and Douglas had a great influence on Elizabeth both as a writer and through his approach to life. At the beginning of the Second World War, she was living on the Greek island of Syros and was evacuated to Egypt, where she ran a reference library for the Ministry of Information in Cairo. Here she met and married Anthony David, an officer in the Indian army. At the end of 1945 she went to join him in New Delhi, but became ill and after some months returned to Britain.

Elizabeth David's first published work, *A Book of Mediterranean Food*, appeared in 1950, but her writing career had begun in the winter of 1946–7, in a hotel in Ross-on-Wye. She had returned to the deprivations of postwar Britain after years of relative plenty in the Middle East and, although the hotel was at least warm, she wrote that the food was "produced with a kind of bleak triumph which amounted almost to a hatred of humanity and humanity's needs." She started to write down her memories of Middle Eastern and Mediterranean cooking, creating a private refuge from the cheerless reality of rationing. In 1949 a friend in the literary world offered to show her collection of notes and recipes to publishers. Most of them thought the idea of a cookbook when there was little food to cook at best absurd, but John Lehmann liked the material and agreed to publish it.

The introduction to *Mediterranean Food* paints a vibrant picture: "The cooking of the Mediterranean shores, endowed with all the natural resources, the color and flavor of the south, is a blend of tradition and brilliant improvisation. The Latin genius flashes from the kitchen pans. It is honest cooking." At that time the ingredients of the Mediterranean lands—olive oil, saffron, garlic, basil, eggplants, figs, pistachio nuts—were hardly to be found in central London, and readers had to rely on memory or imagination to savor Elizabeth's recipes.

These were honest recipes too, collected in Provence, Italy, Corsica, Malta and Greece.

Mediterranean Food was acclaimed as a serious work, with reviewers expressing their belief that once the shortages in Britain were lifted the book would become practical as well as inspirational. The first paperback edition, published in 1955, brought the book to a wide audience at the right time. Rationing had ended in 1954 and Mediterranean imports were beginning to arrive. Many of Elizabeth's dishes were unknown in the Britain of the 1950s, but in a few years foods like paella, moussaka, ratatouille, hummus and gazpacho had become familiar in home kitchens, restaurants and supermarkets throughout the country.

The success of *A Book of Mediterranean Food* was followed in 1951 by *French Country Cooking*, a small book of robust, rustic dishes. In 1960 appeared the more substantial, classic work *French Provincial Cooking*, which dealt with "sober, well-balanced, middle-class French cookery, carried out with care and skill, with due regard to the quality of the materials, but without extravagance or pretension"—a phrase which sums up neatly Elizabeth's own standards. The two French books drew many enthusiasts to France to explore the foods of the countryside "at the riverside inns, the hospitable farmhouses of the Loire and the Dordogne, of Normandy and the Auvergne, in seaport bistros, and occasionally also in *cafés routiers*." Pâtés and terrines, soups enriched with bacon and garlic, meat and poultry stews simmered in wine, and open tarts both savory and sweet found their way into the repertoire of enterprising and creative British cooks. In the 1960s, dinner parties, whether cheap and cheerful or stylish and sophisticated, were often drawn straight from her books.

Meanwhile, Elizabeth had returned to live in Italy for a year, to research and collect material for her third book, *Italian Food*, which came out in 1954. She was one of the first writers to emphasize the importance of regional differences in Italian food. The country was not unified until the later part of the nineteenth century, so to an Italian there was, and is, no such thing as Italian food: "There is Florentine cooking, Venetian cooking, there are the dishes of Genoa, Piedmont, Romagna; of Rome, Naples and the Abruzzi; of Sardinia and Sicily; of Lombardy, Umbria and the Adriatic coast." These provincial differences are clear to every discerning traveller, but at that time found no reflection in the Italian restaurants in Britain; they served up the spaghetti, veal and chicken dishes the British had come to regard as Italian food. Elizabeth then started work on *Summer Cooking*, a smaller and less demanding collection of recipes for simple summer meals, cold buffets and picnics, drawn from old English dishes as well as those of the countries she had travelled in. She concentrated on herbs, fruits and vegetables in season, and on light dishes of poultry or fish.

By 1964 all five books were available in paperback, and they have remained in print

to the present day, with sales into the millions. They found, and continue to find, a large and enthusiastic audience. During the years spent writing the books, Elizabeth also contributed to a variety of newspapers and magazines, having first been commissioned to write a piece entitled "Rice Again" for *Harper's Bazaar* in 1949. At different times she was a regular contributor to *Vogue*, *House and Garden*, the *Sunday Times*, *Wine and Food*, *The Spectator* and *Nova*. Writing for *The Spectator* pleased her most, for there she was allowed to write a column about food, getting away from the standard formula of an introductory paragraph and a clutch of recipes. Her subjects were wide-ranging but topical, with occasional "harmless fun at the expense of restaurant guides or the baiting of public relations persons who made imbecile suggestions."

Elizabeth had a passionate interest in English cooking, and owned a large collection of old English cookery books which she read avidly. From this enthusiasm came the idea for *Spices, Salt and Aromatics in the English Kitchen,* published in 1971. A fine collection of English spiced and aromatic dishes, it revived old treats such as salt duck and spiced beef.

English Bread and Yeast Cookery took five years to write and is the most comprehensive book on English baking. At the time of publication (1977) it had an immense influence. Eighty per cent of the bread sold in Britain came from factories—soft, white and sliced. A revolt against bland, flabby industrial bread was gathering momentum and people were starting to bake their own bread. They seized Elizabeth's bread book and created a demand for flour from small millers, for supplies of yeast, for good bread pans. The industrial loaf is still with us, but look at the wide variety of other breads on sale in supermarkets, delicatessens and from independent bakers, and thank Elizabeth.

Writing was never easy for Elizabeth, yet there is a directness and warmth and an unfailing integrity always present in her work. Her polished style came from writing and rewriting, always by hand, until she was satisfied with the result. She was constantly curious, a stickler for accuracy and the acknowledgement of sources. She had high standards and expected them of others. She detested fuss and anything pretentious or sham. She spoke out about the poor quality of many "factory" foods, about bad restaurants, and condemned writers who published recipes for travesties of traditional dishes.

Elizabeth's recipes make you want to cook; the aroma of a dish and its vibrant colors spring from the page. The instructions may be brief and sometimes sketchy, and were not written in the formulaic style that is considered appropriate today, but they do not let you down. She assumes her readers are intelligent, curious and able to think for themselves. Her writing is clear and authoritative; she tells you the correct way to make a risotto or a pilaf, *ossi buchi* or *bœuf à la bourguignonne*. She wrote as she cooked: with respect for tradition and provenance, with passion and knowledge. She celebrated the pleasures of the table in simple, authentic recipes and evocative essays on the markets of France or Italy, on dishes discovered on her travels, or describing the food of the past.

On both sides of the Atlantic many chefs took up the demand for good-quality ingredients and used her recipes. They continue to acknowledge the debt they owe to Elizabeth David. Many people who do not know her name or her writing have been affected by her influence on chefs and other food writers. Elizabeth was not a public figure, and did not want to be. She chose writing as her means of communicating, and this she did with elegance, erudition, wit and humor. She remains an essential presence in the food world; her writing made it possible for today's celebrity chefs and television supercooks to find a receptive audience.

At Elizabeth David's Table contains a combination of easy, quick recipes that fit well into today's busy schedules, and classic dishes that may take longer but once put together are often left to cook slowly and can be prepared well before the meal. Some recipes are kept in the narrative style, but where there are many ingredients they have been listed at the head of the recipe. Between the recipe chapters are essays on different topics, written over the course of her life. For the first time, the dishes have been photographed, keeping to the same muted colors, earthenware pots and plain white china that Elizabeth describes in her "Dream Kitchen" essay on pages 156–7.

I hope you will enjoy this illustrated collection of recipes from the greatest food writer of our times.

Jill Norman, March 2010

FAST *and* FRESH

It isn't only the expense, the monotony and the false tastes of the food inside most cans and jars and packages which turn me every day more against them. The amount of space they take up, the clutter they make and the performance of opening the things also seem to me quite unnecessarily exasperating. However, even food writers who spend most of their lives with a saucepan in one hand and a pen in the other can't dispense entirely with the kind of stores from which a meal can every now and again be improvised. What I personally require of such things is that there shall be no question whatever of their letting me down or giving me any unwelcome surprise. Out with any product which plays tricks or deteriorates easily. And out also with all the things of which one might say they'll do for an emergency. If something isn't good enough for every day, then it isn't good enough to offer friends, even if they have turned up demanding a meal without notice.

Twenty years ago, during the war years, which I spent in the Eastern Mediterranean, I became accustomed to planning meals from a fairly restricted range of provisions. Now I find myself returning more and more to the same sort of rather ancient and basic foods. They suit my taste and they are the kind of provisions which will always produce a coherent and more or less complete meal, which is just what haphazardly bought cans and packages won't do. What happens when you have to open four cans, two jars and three packets in order to make one hasty cook-up is that you get a thoroughly unsatisfactory meal; and the contents of half-used tins and jars have got to be dealt with next day—or left to moulder in the fridge. The only stores I had to bother about when I lived for a time in a small seashore village on an Ægean island were bread, olive oil, olives, salt fish, hard white cheese, dried figs, tomato paste, rice, dried beans, sugar, coffee and wine.

With fresh fish—mostly small fry or squid, but occasionally a treat such as red mullet or a langouste to be obtained from one of the fisher boys, with vegetables and fruit from the garden of the tavern owner, eggs at about twopence a dozen, and meat—usually kid, lamb or pork—available only for feast days, the diet was certainly limited, but at least presented none of the meal-planning problems which, as I have learned from readers' letters, daily plague the better-off English housewife.

Subsequently, in war-time Egypt, I found, in spite of the comparative plenty and variety and the fact that in Greece I had often grumbled about the food, that the basic commodities of the Eastern Mediterranean shores were the ones which had begun to seem essential. Alexandrians, not surprisingly, knew how to prepare these commodities in a more civilized way than did the Greek islanders. The old-established merchant families of the city—Greek, Syrian, Jewish, English— appeared to have evolved a most delicious and unique blend of Levantine and European cookery and were at the same time most marvellously hospitable. I have seldom seen such wonderfully glamorous-looking, and tasting, food as the Levantine cooks of Alexandria could produce for a party. And yet when you got down to analyzing it, you would find that much the same ingredients had been used in dish after dish—only they were so differently treated, so skilfully blended and seasoned and spiced that each one had its own perfectly individual character and flavor.

In Cairo the dividing line between European and Eastern food was much sharper. It was uphill work trying to make English-trained Sudanese cooks produce interesting food. Most of them held a firm belief that the proper meal to set before English people consisted of roast or fried chicken, boiled vegetables and a dessert known to one and all as grème garamel.

My own cook, Suleiman, was a Sudanese who had previously worked only for Italian and Jewish families. He was erratic and forgetful, but singularly sweet-natured, devoted to his cooking pots and above all knew absolutely nothing of good, clean, English schoolroom food.

I used occasionally to try to teach him some French or English dish for which I had a nostalgic craving, but time for cooking was very limited, my kitchen facilities even more so, and on the whole I left him to his own devices.

So it came about that for three or four more years I lived mainly on rather rough but highly flavored, colorful shining vegetable dishes, lentil or fresh tomato soups, delicious spiced pilafs, lamb kebabs grilled over charcoal, salads with cool mint-flavored yogurt dressings, the Egyptian fellahin dish of black beans with olive oil and lemon and hard-boiled eggs—these things were not only attractive but also cheap and this was important because although Egypt was a land of fantastic plenty compared with war-time Europe, a lot of the better-class food was far beyond the means of young persons living on British Civil Service pay without foreign allowances, and canned goods were out of the question because there was no room for them in the cave which my landlord was pleased to describe as a furnished flat.

What I found out when I returned to England to another five or six years of the awful dreary foods of rationing was that while my own standard of living in Egypt had perhaps not been very high, my food had always had some sort of life, color, guts, stimulus; there had always been bite, flavor and inviting smells. Those elements were totally absent from English meals.

As imports came slowly back, I found once more, and still find, that it is the basic foods of the Mediterranean world which produce them in the highest degree. And it is curious how much more true variety can be extracted from a few of these basic commodities than from a whole supermarketful of products, none of which really taste of anything in particular.

So long as I have a supply of elementary fresh things like eggs, onions, parsley, lemons, oranges and bread and tomatoes—and I keep canned tomatoes too—I find that my pantry will always provide the main part of an improvised meal. If this has to be made quickly it may be just a salad of anchovy fillets and black olives, hard-boiled eggs and olive oil, with bread and a bottle of wine. If it is a question of not being able to leave the house to go shopping, or of being too otherwise occupied to stand over the cooking pots, then there are white beans or brown lentils for slow cooking, and usually a piece of cured sausage or bacon to add to them, with onions and oil and possibly tomato. Apricots or other dried fruit can be baked in the oven at the same time, or I may have oranges for a fruit salad, and if it comes to the worst there'll at least be bread and butter and honey and jam. Or if I am given, say, forty-five minutes to get an unplanned meal ready—well, I have Italian and Patna rice and Parmesan, spices, herbs, currants, almonds, walnuts, to make a risotto or a pilaf. And perhaps tuna, with eggs to make mayonnaise, for an easy first dish. The countless number of permutations to be devised is part of the entertainment.

from The Spectator, *9 December 1960*

STARTERS

and

LIGHT

DISHES

It is very easy to make an attractive first course from vegetables, eggs, shrimp, rice and simple sauces; it is only a question of imagination, and the most elementary knowledge of cooking. The simplest starters are the best, looking clean and fresh. One of the nicest of all is the Genoese one of raw fava beans, rough salami sausage and salty sheep's milk Sardo cheese; each of these things is served on a separate dish, and each person peels his own beans and cuts his own cheese; if the same ingredients were all mixed up together in a bowl the point would be quite lost. In the same way, a salad of tuna piled up on white or green beans dressed with oil has two quite contrasting but compatible flavors, whereas if the tuna is mashed up among the beans, the flavors and textures of both are sacrificed, and the appearance of the dish messy as well.

Apart from all the little dishes which can be cheaply made at home, there are now so many products on the market which make delicious starters. All the smoked fish—trout, mackerel, herring, salmon, sturgeon, eel—need no accompaniment other than lemon, and bread and butter; smoked cod's roe pounded into a paste with olive oil and lemon juice is excellent served with hot toast (eaten straight it is good but disconcertingly sticky).

Among Italian antipasti are to be found some of the most successful culinary achievements in European cooking. The most common antipasti are some kind of salami sausage, olives, anchovies, ham, small artichokes in oil, peppers in oil, raw fennel and raw fava beans. Of varieties of salami there is seemingly no end. Some are garlicky, some not; some are eaten very fresh, others are considered best when they have matured. Prosciutto di Parma and prosciutto San Daniele are at their best perhaps the most delicious hams in the world and the most perfect antipasti. Whose was the brilliant idea of combining fine slices of these hams with fresh figs? Or melon? (Though melons are very much a second best.)

Antipasti of fish, all kinds of small fry served in oil and vinegar sauces, as well as anchovies and the inevitable tuna, are at their best in Italy. Langoustines, scampi, shrimps, seppie, calamaretti, totani, moscadini (the last four are of the squid family), mussels, clams, sea dates, sea truffles, oysters, crabs, cold sturgeon in oil, all appear as starters.

Vegetables are presented in a number of ways, and there are plenty of ideas from which we could borrow. It is the unexpected which makes the charm of many of these little dishes: papery slices of raw artichokes; anchovies garnishing a salad of raw mushrooms; slices of Gruyère cheese with crisp fennel or rounds of uncooked peppers; cooked artichoke hearts mixed into a salad of green peas, fava beans and potatoes; tuna encased in rolled-up peppers. To the enterprising there is no limit to the number of dishes with which, without overdoing the mixtures, a promising start to a meal may be contrived.

PIEDMONTESE PEPPERS

peperoni alla piemontese

Cut some *red, yellow* or *green peppers* in half lengthwise. Take out all the seeds and wash the peppers. If they are large, cut each half in half again. Into each piece put 2 or 3 slices of *garlic*, 2 small sections of raw *tomato*, about half a fillet of *anchovy* cut into pieces, a small nut of *butter*, a teaspoon of *olive oil*, a very little *salt*. Arrange these peppers on a flat baking dish and cook them in a moderate oven at 350°F, for about 30 minutes. They are not to be completely cooked; they should in fact be al dente, the stuffing inside deliciously oily and garlicky.

Serve them cold, each garnished with a little parsley.

Allow ½ or 1 pepper per person.

CORIANDER MUSHROOMS

This is a quickly cooked little dish which makes a delicious cold hors d'œuvre. The aromatics used are similar to those which go into the well-known *champignons à la grecque*, but the method is simpler, and the result even better. In larger quantities the same dish can be made as a hot vegetable to be eaten with veal or chicken.

6oz firm, white, round and very fresh mushrooms, lemon juice, 2 tablespoons olive oil, a teaspoon of crushed coriander seeds, and 1 or 2 bay leaves, salt, freshly ground pepper.

Rinse the mushrooms, wipe them dry with a clean cloth, slice them (but do not peel them) into quarters, or if they are large into eighths. The stems should be neatly trimmed. Squeeze over them a little lemon juice.

In a heavy frying pan or sauté pan, warm the olive oil. Into it put the coriander seeds. Let them heat for a few seconds. Keep the heat low. Put in the mushrooms and the bay leaves. Add the seasoning. Let the mushrooms cook gently for a minute, cover the pan and leave them, still over very low heat, for another 3 to 5 minutes. Cultivated mushrooms should not be cooked for longer than the time specified.

Uncover the pan. Decant the mushrooms—with all their juices—into a shallow serving dish and sprinkle them with fresh olive oil and lemon juice.

Whether the mushrooms are to be served hot or cold do not forget to put the bay leaf which has cooked with them into the serving dish. The combined scents of coriander and bay go to make up part of the true essence of the dish.

Cooked mushrooms do not keep well, but a day or two in the refrigerator does not harm this coriander-spiced dish. It is also worth remembering that uncooked cultivated mushrooms can be stored in a plastic box in the refrigerator and will keep fresh for a couple of days.

Enough for three people.

PROVENÇAL TOMATO SALAD

tomates provençales en salade

Take the stalks off a large bunch of *parsley*; pound the leaves with a little *salt*, in a mortar, with 2 cloves of *garlic* and a little *olive oil*.

Cut the tops off good raw *tomatoes*; with a teaspoon soften the pulp inside, sprinkle with *salt*, and turn them upside down so that the water drains out. Fill the tomatoes up with the parsley and garlic mixture. Serve them after an hour or two, when the flavor of the garlic and parsley has permeated the salad.

TOMATOES *with* CREAM

tomatoes à la crème

Put the required number of whole *tomatoes* into boiling water to remove the skins. Arrange them in a shallow salad bowl.

Pour over them a dressing consisting simply of thick fresh *heavy cream* into which is stirred a little *salt* and a tablespoon of chopped *tarragon* or fresh sweet *basil*.

A splendid accompaniment for a cold or, for that matter, a hot chicken.

Allow 1–2 tomatoes per person.

EGGPLANT PURÉE

This is a Middle Eastern dish which is intended to be served as an hors d'œuvre with bread, or with meat, in the same manner as a chutney.

Grill or bake 4 *eggplants* until their skins crack and will peel easily. Mash the peeled eggplants, mix them with 2 or 3 tablespoons of *yogurt*, the same of *olive oil*, *salt*, *pepper*, *lemon juice*. Garnish with a few very thin slices of raw *onion* and chopped *mint* leaves.

Enough for four people.

EGGPLANT CHUTNEY

Boil 2 *eggplants* in their skins; leave them to get cold. Peel them and put the pulp through a food processor. Stir a crushed clove of *garlic* into the purée, add a little minced *onion*, *green chile* and grated *ginger*, and season with *salt*, *pepper* and *lemon juice*.

Enough for three to four people.

CHICKEN LIVER PÂTÉ

With the exception of the incomparable *pâté de foie gras*, store-bought pâtés are seldom very satisfactory, and it is not difficult to make your own. If you have no earthenware or ovenproof porcelain terrines in which to cook them, this need be no deterrent. For a very small cost enamelled baking pans in all sizes, fireproof glass dishes, or even oblong loaf pans can be bought, and these serve just as well. They don't look quite so nice on the table, but the pâtés can be turned out on to a dish and sliced for serving.

> *1lb chicken livers (or duck, turkey, chicken and goose liver mixed), pork,*
> *duck or goose fat or butter, brandy, port or Madeira, ½ a clove of garlic,*
> *salt and pepper, a small pinch of thyme leaves.*

Clean the livers carefully and pare off any parts of them which look greenish, as they will give a bitter taste to the pâté. Melt 2 tablespoons of butter in a frying pan; put in the livers, whole, and let them cook gently for about 5 minutes. They must remain pink inside. Take them from the pan and put them into a mortar or blender. To the butter in the pan add 2 tablespoons of brandy and let it bubble; then 2 tablespoons of port or madeira, and cook another minute. Add half a clove of garlic, salt, ground black pepper and a small pinch of thyme to the livers and pound or blend them to a paste; pour in the butter mixture from the pan, and 4 tablespoons of fresh butter. When all is thoroughly amalgamated and reduced to a paste, put it into an earthenware terrine in which it will come to within ½ inch of the top.

In a clean pan melt some pure pork, duck or goose fat, or butter. Pour it through a strainer on to the pâté; there should be enough to form a covering about ¼ inch thick, so that the pâté is completely sealed. When the fat has set, cover with a piece of foil and the lid of the terrine. Store in the refrigerator. The pâté should not be eaten until two or three days after it has been made, and as long as it is airtight will keep several weeks in a refrigerator. Serve it very cold, in the terrine, with toast.

This is a rich pâté, and butter is not necessary with it.

1lb of chicken livers makes enough pâté for eight to ten people.

PORK *and* LIVER PÂTÉ
terrine de campagne

This is the sort of pâté you get in French restaurants under the alternative names of *pâté maison* or *terrine du chef*. Serve this pâté as a first course, with toast or French bread. Some people like butter as well, although it is quite rich enough without. An obliging butcher will usually grind for you the pork, veal and liver, provided he is given due notice. It saves a great deal of time, and I always believe in making my dealers work for me if they will.

> *1lb pork belly (without rind), ground, 1lb lean veal, ground, ½lb pig's liver, ground, 4oz sliced bacon or pork back fat, 1 clove of garlic, crushed, 6 black peppercorns, crushed, 6 juniper berries, crushed, 1–2 teaspoon salt, ¼ teaspoon ground mace, 3–4 tablespoons dry white wine, 2 tablespoons brandy.*

To the ground meats, all thoroughly blended, add 2oz of the bacon or pork fat cut in thin, irregular little dice, the garlic and seasonings, and the wine and brandy. Mix very thoroughly and, if there is time, leave to stand for an hour or two before cooking, so that the flavors penetrate the meat. Turn into one large 4-cup capacity terrine, or into 2 or 3 smaller ones, 2½ inches deep. Cut the remaining fat or bacon into thin strips and arrange it across the top of the pâté. Place the terrines in a baking pan half-filled with water and cook, uncovered, in a slow oven, 325°F, for 1¼ to 1½ hours. The pâtés are cooked when they begin to come away from the sides of the dish.

Take them from the oven, being careful not to spill any of the fat, and leave them to cool. They will cut better if, when the fat has all but set, they are weighted. To do this, cover with parchment paper and a board or plate which fits inside the terrine and put a weight on top. However, if this proves impractical, it is not of very great importance. If the terrines are to be kept longer than a week, cover them completely, once they are cold, with a sealing layer of just-melted pure pork lard.

When cooking any pâté remember that it is the depth of the terrine rather than its surface area which determines the cooking time. The seasonings of garlic and juniper berries are optional.

The proportions of meat, liver and seasonings making up a pâté can be altered to suit individual tastes, but always with due regard to the finished texture of the product. A good pâté is moist and fat without being greasy, and it should be faintly pink inside, not grey or brown. A dry pâté is either the result of overcooking, or of too small a proportion of fat meat having been used.

Enough for eight to ten people.

RILLETTES

Rillettes will keep for weeks, and make an excellent standby for an hors d'œuvre. Serve them with bread and white wine.

1½–2lb pork belly, with a good proportion of lean to fat, 1 clove of garlic,
a sprig of fresh thyme or marjoram, salt, pepper, a pinch of ground mace.

Remove bones and rind from the meat, and cut it into small cubes. Put these into a thick pan with the chopped garlic, the herbs and seasoning. Cook on a very low flame, or in the slowest possible oven at 275°F for 1½ hours, until the pieces of pork are quite soft without being fried, and swimming in their own fat. Place a wide sieve over a bowl, and pour the meat into the sieve so that the fat drips through into the bowl. When the meat has cooled, pull it into shreds, using two forks. If you cannot manage this, chop the meat. But unless you are making rillettes in a large quantity, try to avoid using the electric blender. It gives the meat too compact and smooth a texture. Pack the rillettes into small earthenware or china pots, and seal them with their own fat. Cover with parchment paper or foil and refrigerate until serving.

Enough for four to six people.

PORK *and* SPINACH TERRINE

This pâté can be eaten hot as a main course, but I prefer it cold, as a first dish, and with bread or toast just as a pâté is always served in France.

The interesting points about this dish are its appearance, its fresh, uncloying flavor and its comparative lightness, which should appeal to those who find the better-known type of pork pâté rather heavy. You could, for example, serve a quite rich or creamy dish after this without overloading anybody's stomach.

At Orange, that splendid town they call the gateway to Provence, I once tasted a pâté which was more fresh green herbs than meat. I was told that this was made according to a venerable country recipe of Upper Provence. The pâté was interesting but rather heavy. I have tried to make it a little less filling. Here is the result of my experiments.

1lb uncooked spinach or chard, 1lb freshly ground fatty pork, seasonings of salt, freshly ground pepper, mixed spices.

Wash, cook and drain the spinach. When cool, squeeze it as dry as you can. There is only one way to do this—with your hands. Chop it roughly.

Season the meat with 2–3 teaspoons of salt, a generous amount of freshly ground black pepper, and about a ¼ teaspoon of mixed ground spices (mace, allspice, cloves).

Mix the meat and spinach together. Turn into a 2-cup earthenware terrine or loaf pan. On top put a piece of buttered parchment paper. Stand the terrine or pan in a baking dish half filled with water.

Cook in a low oven at 325°F for 45 minutes to an hour. Do not let it get overcooked or it will be dry.

Enough for six to eight people.

FRESH HERBS

The use of herbs in cooking is so much a matter of tradition, almost of superstition, that the fact that it is also a question of personal taste is overlooked, and experiments are seldom tried; in fact the restriction of this herb to that dish is usually quite arbitrary, and because somebody long ago discovered that basil works some sort of spell with tomatoes, fennel with fish, and rosemary with pork, it occurs to few people to reverse the traditional usage; to take an example, fennel is an excellent complement to pork, adding the sharpness which is supplied in English cookery by apple sauce, while basil enhances almost anything with which it is cooked; for ideas one has only to look to the cooking of other countries to see how much the use of herbs as a flavoring can be varied.

In England mint is considered to have an affinity for lamb, new potatoes, and green peas; the French regard the use of mint as a flavoring as yet another sign of English barbarism, and scarcely ever employ it, while all over the Middle East, where the cooking is far from uncivilized, mint is one of the most commonly used of herbs; it goes into soups, sauces, omelettes, salads, purées of dried vegetables and into the sweet cooling mint tea drunk by the Persians and Arabs. In Spain, where the cooking has been much influenced by the Arabs, it is also used in stews and soups; it is usually one of the ingredients of the sweet sour sauces which the Italians like, and which are a legacy from the Romans, and in modern Roman cooking wild mint gives a characteristic flavor to stewed mushrooms and to vegetable soups. The Indians make a fresh chutney from pounded mint, mangoes, onion and chiles, which is an excellent accompaniment to fish and cold meat as well as to curries. Mint is one of the cleanest tasting of herbs and will give a lively tang to many vegetables, carrots, tomatoes, mushrooms, lentils; a little finely chopped mint is good in fish soups and stews, and with braised duck; a cold roast duck served on a bed of freshly picked mint makes a lovely, fresh-smelling summer dish; a few leaves can be added to the orange salad to serve with it.

With its highly aromatic scent, basil is one of the most delicious of all herbs, best known for bringing out the flavor of tomato salads and sauces. In Provence, in Italy, in Greece, basil grows and is used in great quantities. The Genoese could scarcely exist without their pesto, a thick compound of pounded basil, pine nuts, garlic, cheese and olive oil which is used as a sauce for every kind of pasta, for fish, particularly red mullet, and as a flavoring for soups and minestrones. Once you have become a basil addict it is hard to do without it; Mediterranean vegetables such as peppers and eggplants, garlicky soups and wine-flavored dishes of beef, salads dressed with the fruity olive oil of Provence or Liguria and all the dishes with tomato sauces need basil as a fish needs water, and there is no substitute.

Of that very English herb sage I have little to say except that, and this is where the question of personal taste comes in, it seems to me to be altogether too blatant, and used far too much; its all-pervading presence in stuffings and sausages is perhaps responsible for the distaste for herbs which many English people feel. The Italians are also very fond of sage, and use it a great deal with veal and with liver; it seems to give a musty rather than a fresh flavor, and I would always substitute mint or basil for sage in any recipe. The same applies to rosemary, which when fresh gives out a powerful oil which penetrates anything cooked with it; in southern France it is used to flavor roast lamb, pork and veal, but should be removed from the dish before it is served, as it is disagreeable to find those spiky little leaves in one's mouth; in Italy rosemary is stuffed in formidable quantities into roast suckling pig, and in the butchers' shops you see pork roasts tied up ready for roasting wreathed round and threaded with rosemary; it looks entrancing, but if you want to taste the meat, use only the smallest quantity, and never put it into stock destined for a consommé or for a sauce.

Thyme, marjoram and wild marjoram are all good and strong-flavored herbs which can be used separately or together for robust stews of beef in red wine, for those aromatic country soups in which there are onions, garlic, bacon, wine, cabbage; one or other of these herbs should go into stuffings for chicken, goose and turkey, for peppers and eggplants, into meat croquettes (accompanied by grated lemon peel), terrines of game, and stews of hare and rabbit; either thyme or marjoram is almost essential to strew in small quantities on pork and lamb chops and liver to be fried or grilled; wild marjoram is called *origano* in Italy and Spain and is used for any and every dish of veal and pork, for fish and fish soups, and is an essential ingredient of the Neapolitan pizza, that colorful, filling, peasant dish of bread dough baked with tomatoes, anchovies and cheese.

Fennel has many uses besides the sauce for mackerel which is found in all old English cookery books. For the famous Provençal *grillade au fenouil* the sundried, brittle stalks of the fennel are used as a bed on which to grill sea bass (*loup de mer*) or red mullet; there is a Tuscan chicken dish in which the bird is stuffed with thick strips of ham and pieces of fennel bulb and pot-roasted; in Perugia they stuff their suckling pig and pork with fennel leaves and garlic instead of the rosemary prevalent elsewhere in Italy; one of the best of Italian sausages is *finocchiona*, a Florentine pork salami flavored with fennel seeds; if you like the aniseed taste of fennel, use it chopped up raw in soups, particularly iced soups, and in vinaigrette sauces, in rice salads to give the crisp element so necessary to soft foods, in mixed vegetable salads, in fish mayonnaises, in the court-bouillon in which fish is to be poached, in stuffings for baked fish, in chicken salads, and mixed with parsley and juniper berries for a marinade for pork chops which are to be grilled.

Tarragon is essentially a herb of French cookery; *poulet à l'estragon* and *œufs en gelée à l'estragon* are classics of the French kitchen; without tarragon there is no true Sauce Béarnaise; with chives and chervil or parsley it is one of the *fines herbes* for omelettes, sauces, butters, and many dishes of grilled meat and fish. It is an herb to be used with care for its charm lies in its very distinct and odd flavor and too much of it spoils the effect, but a few leaves will give character to many dishes and particularly to smooth foods such as sole cooked in cream, *œufs en cocotte*, cream soups, bisques of shell fish, stewed scallops, potato purées and also to tomato salads. In Italy, tarragon is to be found only in and around Siena, where it is used in the stuffing for globe artichokes, and to flavor green salads.

The quantity in which any given herb is to be used is a matter of taste rather than of rule. Cookery books are full of exhortations to discretion in this matter, but much depends on the herb with which you happen to be dealing, what food it is to flavor, whether the dish in question is to be a long-simmered one in which it is the sauce which will be ultimately flavored with the herbs, or whether the herbs are to go into a stuffing for a bird or meat to be roasted, in which case the aromas will be more concentrated, or again whether the herbs will be cooked only a minute or two, as in egg dishes, or not cooked at all, as when they are used to flavor a salad or an herb butter. Whether the herbs are fresh or dried is an important point. The oils in some herbs (rosemary, wild marjoram, sage) are very strong, and when these dry out the flavor is very much less powerful. But in the drying process nearly all herbs (mint is an exception) acquire a certain mustiness, so that although in theory one should be able to use dried herbs more freely than fresh ones, the opposite is in fact generally the case.

Some fresh herbs disperse their aromatic scent very quickly when in contact with heat; a few leaves of fresh tarragon steeped in a hot consommé for 20 minutes will give it a strong flavor, whereas if the tarragon is to flavor a salad considerably more will be necessary. Lemon thyme and marjoram are at their best raw, or only slightly cooked, as in an omelette; the flavor of fennel stalks is brought out by slow cooking; basil has a particular affinity with all dishes in which olive oil is an ingredient, whether cooked or in salads. Knowledge of the right quantities, and of interesting combinations of herbs, can be acquired by using egg dishes, salads and soups as a background. Even if the herbs have been dispensed with a less cautious hand than is usually advised the result will not be a disaster, as it can be when some musty dried herb has completely permeated a roast bird or an expensive piece of meat. You may, on the contrary, have discovered some delicious new combination of tastes, and certainly the use of fresh herbs will be a startling revelation to all those people who know herbs only as something bought in a packet called "mixed dried herbs," and for which you might just as well substitute sawdust.

from Summer Cooking, *1955*

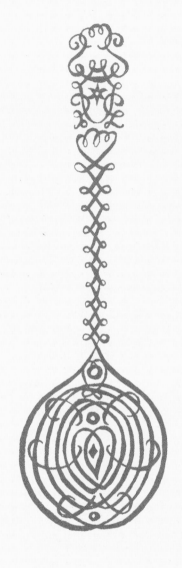

SOUPS

The making of a good soup is quite an art, and many otherwise clever cooks do not possess the *tour de main* necessary to its successful preparation. Either they over-complicate the composition of the dish, or they attach only minor importance to it, reserving their talents for the meal itself, and so it frequently happens that the soup does not correspond in quality to the rest of the dishes; nevertheless, the quality of the soup should foretell that of the entire meal.

Madame Seignobos, who wrote these words some fifty years ago in a book called *Comment on forme une cuisinière*, was probably referring to trained cooks, and does not mention those other happy-go-lucky ones who tell you, not without pride, "of course I never follow a recipe, I just improvise as I go along. A little bit of this, a spoonful of that . . . it's much more fun really." Well, it may be more fun for the cook, but is seldom so diverting for the people who have to eat his products, because those people who have a sure enough touch to invent successfully in the kitchen without years of experience behind them are very rare indeed. The fortunate ones gifted with that touch are those who will also probably have the restraint to leave well alone when they have hit on something good; the ones who can't resist a different little piece of embroidery every time they cook a dish will end by inducing a mood of gloomy apprehension in their families and guests. The domain of soup-making is one which comes in for more than its fair share of attention from the "creative" cook, a saucepan of innocent-looking soup being a natural magnet to the inventive, and to those who pride themselves on their gifts for inspired improvisation.

I remember when I was very young being advised by the gastronomic authority among my contemporaries to take pretty well everything in the larder, including the remains of the salad (if I remember rightly, some left-over soused herring was also included), tip it into a pan, add some water, and in due course, he said, some soup would emerge. I very soon learned, from the results obtained by this method, that the soup pot cannot be treated as though it were a dustbin. That lesson was elementary enough. The ones that are harder to assimilate are, first, in regard to the wisdom or otherwise of mixing too many ingredients, however good, to make one soup; the likelihood is that they will cancel each other out, so that although your soup may be a concentrated essence of good and nourishing ingredients, it will not taste of anything in particular. Secondly, one has to learn in the end that the creative urge in the matter of embellishments is best kept under control. If your soup is already very good of its kind, possessed of its own true taste, will it not perhaps be spoilt by the addition of a few chopped olives, of a little piece of diced sausage, of a spoonful of paprika pepper? These are matters which everyone must decide for himself.

GAZPACHO

Gazpacho, the popular iced Spanish soup, was described, somewhat disparagingly, by the novelist Théophile Gautier in his *Un Voyage en Espagne* (translated by Catherine Alison Phillips) after a journey to Spain in 1840; like all good Frenchmen he was apt to be suspicious of foreign food.

> Our supper was of the simplest kind; all the serving men and maids of the hostelry had gone to the dance, and we had to be content with a mere gaspacho. This gaspacho is worthy of a special description, and we shall here give the recipe. You pour some water into a soup tureen, and to this water you add a dash of vinegar, some cloves of garlic, some onions cut into quarters, some slices of cucumber, a few pieces of pimento, a pinch of salt; then one cuts some bread and sets it to soak in this pleasing mixture, serving it cold. It is the favorite dish of the Andalusians, and the prettiest women do not shrink from swallowing bowlfuls of this hell-broth of an evening. Gaspacho is considered highly refreshing, an opinion which strikes me as rather rash, but, strange as it may seem the first time one tastes it, one ends by getting used to it and even liking it.

Modern versions of gazpacho appear to be very different from the hell-broth described by Gautier. The basis of them is chopped tomato, olive oil, and garlic, and there may be additions of cucumber, black olives, raw onion, red pepper, herbs, a couple of coarsely chopped hard-boiled eggs, and bread. Sometimes a selection of the vegetables—the cucumber, olives, peppers, onions—and the bread, are finely chopped and handed round separately in small dishes instead of being incorporated in the basic soup.

Chop 1lb raw peeled *tomatoes* until they are almost in a purée. Stir in a few dice of *cucumber*, 2 chopped cloves of *garlic*, a finely sliced *scallion*, a dozen pitted *black olives*, a few strips of *green pepper*, 3 tablespoons of *olive oil*, a tablespoon of *wine vinegar*, *salt*, *pepper* and a pinch of *cayenne pepper*, a little chopped fresh *marjoram*, *mint*, or *parsley*. Keep very cold until it is time to serve the soup, then thin with 1¼ cups of iced water, add a few cubes of coarse *whole wheat bread*, and serve with broken-up ice floating in the bowl.

Sometimes gazpacho is presented in large deep cups, sometimes in shallow soup plates.

Enough for four people.

FRESH GREEN PEA SOUP

2 tablespoons butter, half a small onion, 1oz ham, ¾ cup shelled green peas,
salt, pepper, sugar, mint, ¼ cup heavy cream, 2 eggs, the juice of a lemon,
3¾ cups veal or chicken stock.

In a heavy saucepan, melt the butter; put in the finely chopped onion. Do not let it brown, only soften. Add the ham cut into strips, then the peas. Let them get thoroughly impregnated with the butter. Season with salt, pepper, sugar, and add a little sprig of mint. Pour over hot water just to cover and simmer until the peas are tender. Stir in boiling cream. Remove from the fire and stir in the eggs beaten up with the lemon juice. Pour the boiling stock over this mixture, stirring all the time, or the soup will curdle. Serve at once. A lovely soup.

Enough for four people.

TOMATO SOUP
minestra di pomidoro

In the summer this soup can be eaten iced, accompanied by hot crostini.

In a heavy saucepan, melt 1½lb chopped and skinned *tomatoes* in *olive oil*; add a clove of *garlic* and some fresh *parsley* or *basil* or *marjoram*. Cook for 5 minutes, then add 2½ cups *meat or chicken stock*, *salt* and *pepper*, and a pinch of *sugar*. Cook for 5 minutes more only. By this method the flavor of the tomatoes is retained, and the soup tastes very fresh.

Enough for four people.

VEGETABLE *and* HERB SOUP
purée léontine

Léontine was the young cook of the French family in Paris with whom I lived when I was sixteen. Her food was beautiful.

> *2lb leeks, ⅓ cup good-quality olive oil, salt and pepper, 1 lemon, 1 cup each*
> *of spinach, shelled green peas and shredded lettuce, 1 tablespoon each of*
> *chopped parsley, mint and celery.*

Clean and cut the leeks into chunks. Into a thick-bottomed saucepan put the olive oil and when it is warm put in the leeks, seasoned with salt, pepper and the juice of ½ the lemon. Simmer slowly for about 20 minutes. Now add the spinach, the peas and the lettuce, stir a minute or two, and add 5 cups of water. Cook until all the vegetables are soft—about 10 minutes—then press the whole mixture through a sieve. If the purée is too thick add a little milk, and before serving taste and add more lemon juice if necessary. Stir in the chopped parsley, mint and celery.

This soup turns out an appetizing pale green.

Enough for six people.

MUSHROOM SOUP
potage aux champignons à la bressane

This is an old-fashioned way of making mushroom soup in which bread rather than flour is used for the slight amount of thickening needed. It is a soup with a very fine flavor, but it does need some sort of mild chicken, veal or beef stock.

> *A thick slice of crustless white bread, 4¼ cups veal or chicken stock, ¾lb mushrooms, 4 tablespoons butter, 1 clove of garlic, parsley, salt and pepper, nutmeg or mace, ⅓–½ cup heavy cream.*

Soak the bread in a little of the stock. Rinse the mushrooms in cold water and wipe them dry and free of grit with a soft damp cloth. Do not peel them or remove the stems. Cut them in small pieces. Melt the butter in a heavy saucepan, put in the mushrooms and let them soften; when the moisture starts to run add a very small piece of garlic, chopped, a tablespoon of chopped parsley, a little salt, freshly ground pepper, grated nutmeg or mace, and let the mushrooms continue to stew in the butter for several minutes.

Now squeeze the moisture out of the bread and add the bread to the mushrooms. Stir until it amalgamates with the mushrooms. Add the stock, and cook for about 15 minutes until the mushrooms are quite soft. Put the soup through the coarse mesh of a food mill, then through the next finest one. Or pureé the soup in a blender. You will not get the thick or smooth purée usually associated with mushroom soup, but rather a mixture of the consistency of thin cream broken by all the minuscule particles of the mushrooms. Return it to the rinsed-out saucepan and when it is reheated boil the cream and add to the soup with another tablespoon of parsley, this time chopped very fine indeed.

Enough for four people.

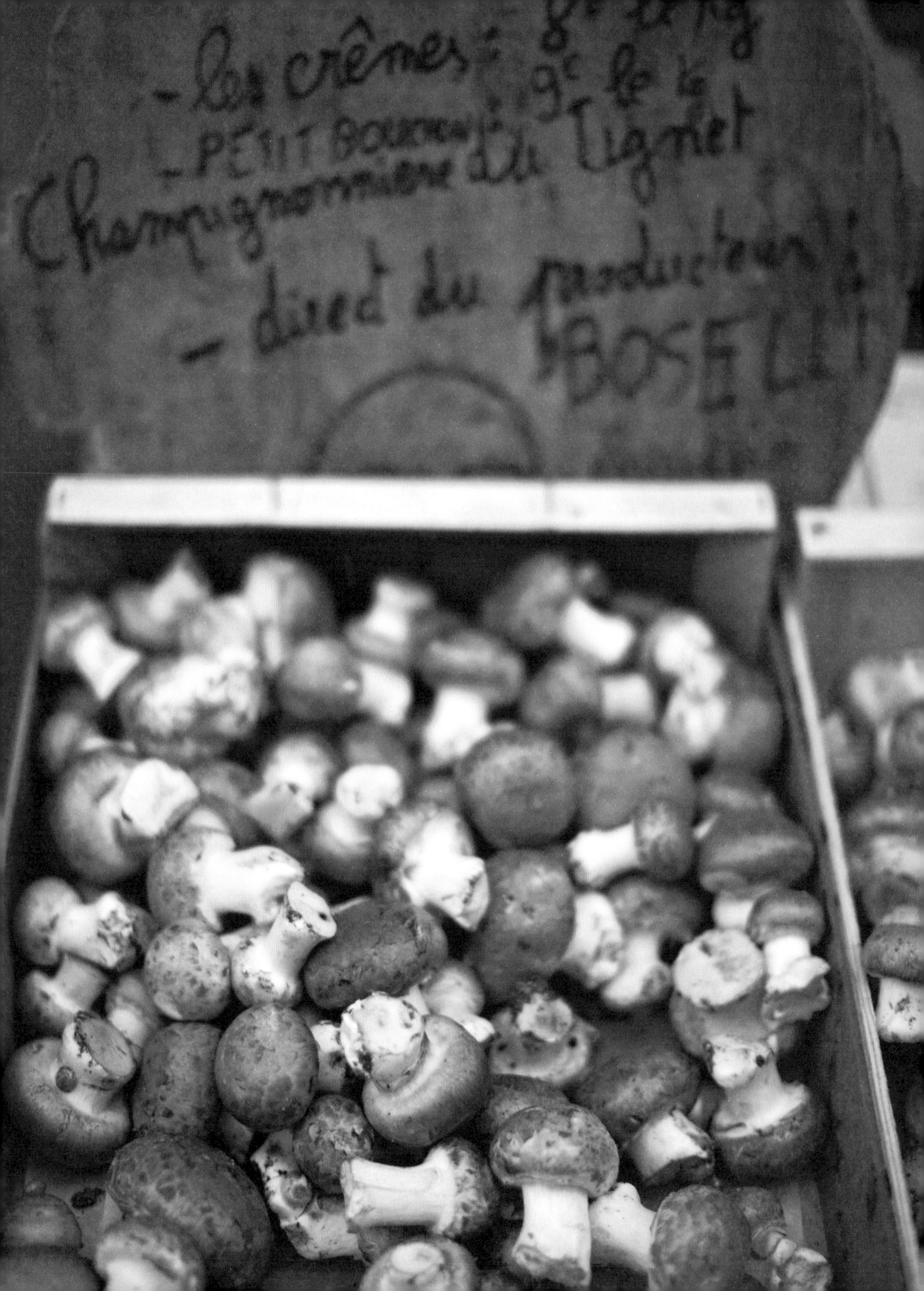
Champignonnière du Lignet
direct du producteur

JERUSALEM
ARTICHOKE SOUP

potage de topinambours à la provençale

Chop up 2lb of peeled *Jerusalem artichokes* and cook in 7 cups of salted water until tender. Drain. Rub through a sieve, and heat up, adding gradually 1¼ cups of *milk*.

In a small frying pan heat 2 tablespoons of *olive oil* and in this fry 2 chopped *tomatoes*, a clove of *garlic*, a small rib of *celery*, chopped, a little *parsley* and 2 tablespoons of chopped *ham or bacon*. Let this mixture cook only a minute or two, then pour it, with the oil, into the soup. Heat, and serve quickly.

Enough for four people.

ZUCCHINI
and TOMATO SOUP
soupe menerboise

½lb zucchini, salt, olive oil, 2 onions, 1lb tomatoes, 2 small potatoes, a handful of shelled and peeled fava beans, ⅓ cup small pasta, pepper, several cloves of garlic, fresh basil, 2 egg yolks, Parmesan cheese.

Cut the zucchini into squares, salt them lightly, and leave them in a colander for an hour so that some of the water drains from them. In an earthenware casserole warm 5 tablespoons of olive oil. Into this put the sliced onions and let them melt but not fry. Add the zucchini and let them melt in the oil slowly for 10 minutes before adding all but 2 of the tomatoes, roughly chopped. When these have softened put in the potatoes cut into small squares and pour about 5 cups of hot water over the whole mixture. Simmer gently for 10 minutes until the potatoes are nearly cooked; then add the fava beans, the pasta and seasoning of salt and pepper.

In the meantime broil the remaining tomatoes, remove their skins; in a mortar pound the garlic, then the tomatoes, and a small bunch of basil. Add the egg yolks, so that you have a sauce somewhat resembling a thin mayonnaise. The pasta in the soup being cooked, stir a ladleful of the soup into the sauce, then another. Return the mixture to the pan, and let it heat gently without boiling, stirring all the time to prevent the egg curdling. At the last minute stir in 2 large spoonfuls of grated Parmesan cheese.

A substantial soup for four to six people.

SPICED LENTIL SOUP

An interesting soup, oriental in flavor, very easy to make, cheap and a comforting standby on which many variations can be made.

Basic ingredients are ⅔ cup red lentils and 2 celery stalks. Others, which can be varied, are 1 small onion, 2 large or 4 small cloves of garlic, 2 teaspoons of cumin seeds (either whole or ground), 1 teaspoon of ground cinnamon, olive oil or butter, water or stock, salt, parsley or dried mint, lemon juice.

In a soup pot, saucepan or casserole of not less than 3½-quart capacity, warm about 6 tablespoons of clarified butter, ghee, or light olive oil or 3 tablespoons of butter. In this melt the chopped onion. Stir in the spices. Let them warm thoroughly before adding the crushed garlic cloves and then the lentils—it is not necessary to soak them—and the celery, cleaned and cut into 2-inch chunks.

Let the lentils soak up the oil or butter before pouring over them 6 cups of water or stock, which could be made from lamb, veal, pork, beef, chicken, turkey or duck. No salt at this stage. Cover the pot and let the lentils cook steadily, but not at a gallop, for 30 minutes. Now throw in 2 teaspoons of salt or to taste and cook for another 15 minutes.

By this time the lentils should be completely soft. It will be a matter of moments to pass them through a food mill or purée them in the blender. I prefer the former method.

Return the soup to a clean saucepan, and when it is reheated, taste for seasoning—it may need a little extra ground cumin and perhaps a sprinkling of cayenne pepper—stir in a tablespoon or two of chopped parsley, or a little dried mint. Lastly, a good squeeze of lemon juice.

Enough for four to six people.

SPICED LENTIL SOUP (2)

As above, but instead of cinnamon and cumin use 1 teaspoon of garam masala, and 1 teaspoon of whole cumin seeds. (The cardamom in the garam masala mixture makes the whole difference to the flavor.) For those who do not mind a rough soup, it is not even necessary to sieve the lentils or whizz them in a blender. Just beat them to a purée with a wooden spoon or a whisk. In this case, it is best to cook the lentils with 1 quart water only and to add broth when they are cooked and reduced to a purée.

Enough for four to six people.

MUSSEL SOUP

zuppa di cozze

This is only one of the many ways of making a mussel soup. Other shellfish can be added, such as large shrimp, allowing 2 or 3 for each person, but they should be bought uncooked, and the tails slit down the center before adding them to the soup.

> *Olive oil, 1 onion, celery, garlic, fresh marjoram, thyme or basil, ground pepper, 2lb tomatoes, white wine, 4 dozen mussels, parsley, lemon peel, bread.*

Cover the bottom of a large and fairly deep pan with olive oil. When it is warm put in the onion, sliced very thinly. As soon as it begins to brown add a tablespoon of chopped celery, 3 cloves of garlic, sliced, some fresh marjoram, thyme or basil, and ground black pepper (no salt). When this has cooked a minute or two put in the skinned and sliced tomatoes and let them stew 3 or 4 minutes before adding a glass of white wine (about ½ cup). Let all bubble 2 minutes before covering the pan and turning down the flame.

Cook until the tomatoes are almost reduced to pulp, then pour in about a cup of hot water, enough to make the mixture about the consistency of a thick soup, and leave to simmer a few more minutes. The basis of the soup is now ready. (It can be prepared beforehand.)

The final operations must be carried out only immediately before serving. Heat the prepared soup and add the carefully cleaned and bearded mussels. Let them cook fairly fast until all are opened, which will take 10–12 minutes. Before serving sprinkle some cut parsley and a scrap of grated lemon peel over the mussels; have ready 3 or 4 slices of toasted French bread for each person, and a large bowl on the table to receive the empty shells as the mussels are eaten.

Enough for four people.

CONFORT ANGLAIS, FRENCH FARE

How gloriously different a matter is French food when you can buy and cook it yourself from that offered at the restaurant meals imposed when you stay in hotels, was brought home to me most forcibly in the early months of 1984. With a friend I was lent, by another and mutual friend, a charming town house in the little south-western city of Uzès. With high ceilings, tall windows, comfortable bedrooms, a bathroom for each, blessedly hot water, central heating, simple and appropriate furniture, good lighting, a large kitchen, electric kettles wherever needed, shelves filled with weeks and weeks of reading, plus all the necessary maps and guide books, the whole place was the most engaging possible blend of traditional French building with unaggressive modern English comforts.

Two minutes' walk from the house was one of those small-town casinos, emporiums of modest size and indeed modest content, but efficiently run, open long hours of every day and providing many of the necessities of life, from butter to electric light bulbs, mineral water to toilet paper, a selection of wines, spirits and liqueurs, adequate cheeses, vegetables, fruit and salad stuffs. Across the road were the food shops, a butcher, a charcuterie, a greengrocery, the market place, the Crédit Lyonnais. Three doors down from the house a fine small bakery provided fresh bread six days a week. As well as everyday baguettes and other white loaves, we had a choice of four or five different varieties of brown bread, including rye and *pain biologique*, France's version of the loaf made from organically grown whole wheat, in this case a very great improvement on the equivalent product of the English health-food shop. As well as good bread the little bakery offered takeaway temptations such as flaky pastry turnovers filled with *brandade de morue*, the creamed salt cod of the region, and an old-fashioned Provençal pissaladière baked in rectangular iron trays and sold by the slice. They call it pizza now. People have forgotten the old name, and will tell you it comes from Italy. I can tell them it comes from no nearer Italy than Marseille where I used to buy it when I lived on a boat tied up in the Vieux Port. That was 1939, before the war started. I used to go ashore every morning and walk up a narrow street to a bakery to buy my pissaladière fresh out of the oven. It was a treat to find my anchovy-and-tomato-spread pissaladière once again in Uzès, and even handier to the house than the Marseille bakery had been to my boat.

Market day at Uzès is Saturday morning. It was February when I was there, not the most propitious time of year for fresh produce, and on the first Saturday of my stay the mistral was blowing so ferociously that it was difficult to stand up. Even the hardy stallholders were shivering and anxious to pack up and climb into the shelter of their vans. Nevertheless, even on a day like that we could buy quite a good variety of vegetables and salads. Among the greatest pleasures, as always in France, were the good creamy-fleshed firm potatoes. Then, even in February, there were little round, crisp, bronze-flecked, frilly lettuces, baskets of mesclun or mixed salad greens, great floppy bunches of chard, leaf artichokes, trombone-shaped pumpkins which make admirable soup, fat fleshy red peppers, new-laid eggs, eight or nine varieties of olives in basins and barrels, thick honey and clear honey, in a variety of colors, in jars and in the comb, and honey soap in golden chunks, bouquets of mixed fresh flowers, tulips, dark purple anemones, marigolds. And then cheeses, cheeses. There are the locally made goats' milk cheeses called *pélardons*, small round and flattish and to be bought in various stages of maturity. Is it for immediate consumption, do you wish to keep it a few days, is it for toasting, roasting, grilling? Try the *magnane à la sarriette*, another goat cheese, strewn with the savory leaves they call *poivre d'âne* across the Rhône in Provence. Or how about the St Marcellin? Or the fresh ewes' milk cheeses? "They are my own," says the lady on the stall. We buy two. They are delicious, but they are horribly expensive, as anyone who has a taste for Roquefort well knows.

Given the very small yield of milk, about a pint per milking, all ewes' milk cheese is a luxury. Here we are not all that far from the place where that great and glorious Roquefort is produced and matured, and in Uzès market, from another cheese stall, we have our pick of three or four grades. Within two or three minutes we have spent £7.00 and have not yet bought our Parmesan or Gruyère for grating onto the delicate little ravioli we have bought from the goat cheese lady. They are tiny, these ravioli, filled with a mixture of parsley and comté, the Gruyère-like cheese of Franche Comté. They take one minute to cook, warns the lady. She imports them from the other side of the Rhône, from Royans near Romans in the Drôme where ravioli have long been a local speciality.

By now we have nearly finished our shopping. We have bought as much as we can carry. But we spend another pound's worth of francs on one of the goat cheese lady's specialities, one of her own. It is something she calls a *tourte à la crème*, or *tourteau*. It is a light, puffy, yeast-leavened tourte, round, like an outsize bun, with a layer of subtly flavored sweet, creamy cream cheese in the center, and with a characteristically blackened top. It is deliberate, this charred top, and traditional, says the lady.

Lunch is going to be a feast. Our red peppers are to be impaled on the electric spit and roasted until their skins are charred as black as the top of the *tourteau*. Then we shall peel them, cut them in strips, dress them with the good olive oil we have bought direct from the little oil mill at Bédarrides on the Tarascon road out of Fontvieille. Over them we strew chopped parsley and garlic and leave them to mature in their dressing. We shall eat them after we have had our bowls of hot ravioli, cooked one minute, according to instructions, in a good chicken broth made from the carcass of a spit-roasted, corn-fed chicken we had a couple of days ago. With fresh brown bread—it always has a good crackly crust—our *sarriette*-strewn *magnane* and a nice creamy little St Marcellin, plus a hunk of that excellent *tourteau* with our coffee, we marvel for the twentieth time in a week that we have such a remarkable choice of provisions here. Pâtés and terrines, large jars of freshly made fish stock, saddle of rabbit rolled and stuffed, ready for roasting or baking, good sausages and *cayettes*, green with the chard so much loved in Rhône Valley cooking, skilfully cut and enticingly trimmed lamb and beef, all the good things from the bakery, the fresh eggs which really are fresh (one stallholder was apologetic because his were three days old), all play their part in making every meal a treat as well as extraordinarily simple to prepare. And in how many towns of no more than 7,500 inhabitants can one choose, on market day, from about seventy different kinds of cheese, at least sixty-five of them French, the rest Italian, Swiss and Dutch?

I must add that Lawrence Durrell, who lives not far away, and who I hadn't seen for a long while, reminded me that many years ago, about 1950, he and I happened to meet in Nîmes and that I complained angrily about the local food, swearing that I would never go back to the region. The area was indeed then very poor. Now the tourists, foreign residents, enterprising wine-growers, motorways, have made it prosperous. Well, there are worse things than words to eat.

from An Omelette and a Glass of Wine, *1984, revised February 1986*

EGGS

"They reckon 685 ways of dressing eggs in the French kitchen; we hope our half-dozen recipes give sufficient variety for the English kitchen." Doctor William Kitchiner, who wrote these words in *The Cook's Oracle*, round about 1821, therewith betrays himself as a pretty smug fellow. For the life of me I cannot see why, if our neighbors twenty-one miles across the Channel have 685 ways of cooking eggs, we should have to make do with six. Six recipes would no more than cover the basic ways of egg cookery common to all countries, but Dr. Kitchiner was certainly right in so far as it is important to understand these methods thoroughly before embarking on the 679 remaining variations.

"Have ready 12 freshly poached eggs," says the cookery book, and with a shudder you turn over the page, knowing that, allowing for disasters, those twelve eggs will probably turn into twenty and that your kitchen will be a charnel house of eggshells and a shambles of running egg yolks. Or "shell 8 *œufs mollets*," they say, "lay each in a puff pastry case and mask with a hollandaise sauce. Pour a cordon of melted meat glaze round each egg and brown with a salamander." And one begins to agree with old Dr. Kitchiner. For elaborate dishes of this sort are not really to be recommended for household cookery.

There are still plenty of lovely egg dishes of a much simpler kind to be made at home; with constant practice and given the time, it is perfectly possible to poach a few eggs successfully; an omelette is very easy to make in spite of all the talk about light hands and heavy frying pans.

Eggs in their own right, as well as all those allied dishes such as the onion tarts of Alsace, the cream and bacon quiches of Lorraine and all the various cheese and egg, potato and cream, and hot pastry confections of different provinces of France make the best possible dishes to serve for a first course or for a simple meal. But it cannot be claimed that these are particularly light dishes. Eggs, and especially eggs with cheese or cream, are very filling. So if you are starting with an onion tart, or a *pipérade*, it is best to make the second course something not too rich, and certainly not one requiring an egg or cream sauce. Egg dishes have a kind of elegance, a freshness, an allure, which sets them quite apart from any other kind of food, so that it becomes a great pleasure to be able to cook them properly and to serve them in just the right condition.

TIAN *with* SPINACH *and* POTATOES

This is one version—entirely my own and a much simplified one—of a Provençal country dish called a *tian*. The *tian* takes its name from the round earthenware gratin dish used for its cooking; and the ingredients which go into it are variable and very much dependent upon individual taste as well as upon family and local tradition.

Green vegetables and eggs are the constants. Tomatoes are almost inevitable, rice or potatoes are quite frequently included. And the *tian* is, like the Spanish omelette or tortilla and the Italian frittata, very often eaten cold as a picnic dish, or as a first—or only—course for the summer midday meal.

When mixing the *tian* ingredients, it's preferable that the vegetables be hot when they are mixed with the beaten eggs, and it is important that as soon as the mixture is ready it be poured into the cooking dish and transferred immediately to the oven. If it is kept waiting in the dish, the eggs tend to rise to the top, so you get a dish in two layers, instead of one integrated and nicely marbled cake.

> *8–11½oz potatoes boiled in their skins, olive oil, salt and pepper, 1lb fresh spinach, garlic, anchovy fillets, 5–6 eggs, 2–3 tablespoons grated Parmesan or Gruyère cheese.*

First peel the cooked potatoes. Cut them in cubes, put them in an earthenware dish (8½ inches) with 2 tablespoons of olive oil and seasonings of salt and pepper. Let them warm in the uncovered dish in a low oven at 300°F while you wash the spinach and cook it very briefly in just the water clinging to the leaves. Season with a little salt. Drain and squeeze dry. Chop it roughly, adding a little garlic if you like, and half a dozen anchovy fillets torn into short lengths. Stir this mixture into the beaten eggs and cheese, then add the cubed potatoes.

Tip the whole mixture into the dish, sprinkle the top with a little oil, return it, uncovered, to the oven, now heated to 375°F. Leave the tian to bake for 25–30 minutes until it is well and evenly risen.

A few pine nuts make a delicious and characteristic addition to this *tian*. An alternative to the potatoes is cooked rice. Allow about ½ cup uncooked rice, for this size of *tian*.

Enough for four people.

TIAN *of* ZUCCHINI

Please do not be daunted by the length of the recipe which follows. Once this dish has been mastered—and it is not at all difficult—you find that you have learned at least three dishes as well as a new way of preparing and cooking zucchini.

The quantities given should be enough for four people but the proportions are deliberately somewhat vague because the *tian* is essentially a dish to be made from the ingredients you have available. If, for instance, you have ½lb only of zucchini, make up the bulk with 4 tablespoons of cooked rice, or the same bulk in diced cooked potatoes.

> *1lb zucchini, salt, 1lb fresh tomatoes, 1 small onion, 2 cloves of garlic, about 1 cup Italian canned whole peeled tomatoes and their juice, fresh basil when in season, and in the winter dried French marjoram or tarragon, 4 large eggs, a handful (i.e. about 3 tablespoons) of grated Parmesan or Gruyère cheese, a handful of coarsely chopped parsley, freshly ground pepper, nutmeg. For cooking the zucchini and tomatoes, a mixture of butter and olive oil.*

To prepare the zucchini, wash them and pare off any parts of the skins which are blemished, leaving them otherwise unpeeled. Slice them lengthwise into four, then cut them into ½-inch chunks. Put them at once into a heavy frying pan or enamelled cast-iron skillet or gratin dish, sprinkle them with salt, and set them without fat of any kind over a very low flame. Watch them carefully, and when the juices, brought out by the salt, start to seep out, turn the zucchini with a spatula, and drop into the pan 2 tablespoons of butter, then a tablespoon or two of olive oil. Cover the pan, and leave the zucchini over a low heat to soften.

While the zucchini are cooking prepare the tomatoes. Pour boiling water over them, skin them, chop them roughly. Peel and chop the onion. Heat a very little butter or olive oil in a pan. First melt the chopped onion without letting it brown. Then put in the tomatoes, season them, add the peeled and crushed garlic. Cook, uncovered, over low heat until a good deal of the moisture is evaporated. Now add the canned tomatoes. These, and their juices, give color, body and the necessary sweetness to the sauce. Sprinkle in the herb of your choice, let the tomato mixture cook until it is beginning to reduce and thicken.

Now amalgamate the zucchini and the tomato mixture. Turn them into a buttered or oiled earthenware gratin dish. For the quantities given, use one of approximately 7-inch diameter and 2-inch depth.

Put the gratin dish, covered with a plate if it has no lid of its own, in a moderate oven, 350°F, for about half an hour, until the zucchini are quite tender.

To finish the *tian*, beat the eggs very well with the cheese, add plenty of seasonings (don't forget the nutmeg) and the coarsely chopped parsley.

Amalgamate the eggs and the vegetable mixture, increase the heat of the oven to 375°F, and leave the *tian* to cook until the eggs are set, risen in the dish, and beginning to turn golden on the top. The time varies between 15 and 25 minutes depending on various factors such as the depth of the dish, the comparative density of the vegetable mixture, the freshness of the eggs, and so on.

When the *tian* is to be eaten cold, leave it to cool in its dish before inverting it onto a serving dish or plate. It should turn out into a very beautiful-looking cake, well-risen and moist. For serving cut it in wedges. Inside, there will be a mosaic of pale green and creamy yellow, flecked with the darker green of the parsley and the red-gold of the tomatoes.

To transport a *tian* on a picnic, it can be left in its cooking dish, or turned out onto a serving plate. Whichever way you choose, cover the tian with parchment paper and another plate, then tie the whole arrangement in a clean white cloth to cradle it during transport.

Enough for four people.

OMELETTES

As everybody knows, there is only one infallible recipe for the perfect omelette: your own. Reasonably enough; a successful dish is often achieved by quite different methods from those advocated in the cookery books or by the professional chefs, but over this question of omelette-making, professional and amateur cooks alike are particularly unyielding. Argument has never been known to convert anybody to a different method, so if you have your own, stick to it and let others go their cranky ways, mistaken, stubborn and ignorant to the end.

It is therefore to anyone still in the experimental stage that I submit the few following points which I fancy are often responsible for failure when that ancient iron omelette pan, for twenty years untouched by water, is brought out of the cupboard.

First, the eggs are very often beaten too savagely. In fact, they should not really be beaten at all, but stirred, and a few firm turns with two forks do the trick. Secondly, the simplicity and freshness evoked by the delicious word "omelette" will be achieved only if it is remembered that it is the eggs which are the essential part of the dish; the filling, being of secondary importance, should be in very small proportion to the eggs. Lying lightly in the center of the finished omelette, rather than bursting exuberantly out of the seams, it should supply the second of two different tastes and textures; the pure egg and cooked butter taste of the outside and ends of the omelette, then the soft, slightly runny interior, with its second flavoring of cheese or ham, mushrooms or fresh herbs.

As far as the pan is concerned, a 10-inch omelette pan will make an omelette of 3 or 4 eggs. Beat them only immediately before you make the omelette, lightly as described above, with two forks, adding a light mild seasoning of salt and pepper. Allow about 1 tablespoon of butter. Warm your pan, don't make it red hot. Then turn the burner as high as it will go. Put in the butter and when it has melted and is on the point of turning color, pour in the eggs. Add the filling, and see that it is well embedded in the eggs. Tip the pan towards you and with a fork or spatula gather up a little of the mixture from the far side. Now tip the pan away from you so that the unset eggs run into the space you have made for them.

When a little of the unset part remains on the surface the omelette is done. Fold it in three with your fork or spatula, hold the pan at an angle and slip the omelette out onto the waiting dish. This should be warmed, but only a little, or the omelette will go on cooking.

An omelette is nothing to make a fuss about. The chief mistakes are putting in too much of the filling and making this too elaborate. Such rich things as foie gras or lobster in cream sauce are inappropriate. In fact, moderation in every aspect is the best advice where omelettes are concerned. Sauces and other trimmings are superfluous, a little extra butter melted in the warm omelette dish or placed on top of the omelette as you serve it being the only addition which is not out of place.

OMELETTE *with* HERBS
omelette fines herbes

Prepare I tablespoon of mixed finely chopped *parsley*, *tarragon*, *chives* and, if possible, *chervil*. Mix half of this, with *salt* and *pepper*, in the bowl with the *eggs*, and add the other half when the eggs are in the pan. If you like, put a little knob of *butter* on top of the omelette as it is brought to the table.

TOMATO OMELETTE
omelette à la tomate

One *tomato*, skinned and chopped small, cooked hardly more than a minute in *butter*, with *salt* and *pepper*, is added to the eggs already in the pan.

BACON OMELETTE
omelette au lard

Add a tablespoon of finely chopped *bacon* softened a minute or so in its own fat, to the *eggs* already in the pan; take care not to salt the eggs too much.

Enough for one person.

SPANISH OMELETTE
tortilla

A Spanish tortilla is a thick, unfolded omelette, consisting only of eggs, potatoes and season- ings. It is cooked in olive oil, should be compact and have almost the appearance of a cake, can be eaten hot or cold, and makes a splendid picnic dish, especially for a car journey. A big tortilla will keep moist for three days.

The following recipe, in note form, is exactly as I wrote it down while watching Juanita, the village girl who once cooked for the photographer Anthony Denney in his house in the province of Alicante. The notes seem to me to convey the essential points about making a tortilla more vividly than would a conventional recipe, and I have used them often without in any way altering the method, except to cook the potatoes rather more gently than Juanita did—she was never a patient girl.

About 1lb potatoes for 4 eggs, oil, garlic, salt. Use an 8½-inch or 9½-inch pan.

Potatoes all cut up small. Soaked in plenty of water (like for Gratin Dauphinois).

Cooked in olive oil (she lets it smoke) in shallow earthenware dish directly on the gas burner. Tiny piece of garlic. Stirred fairly often, and pressed with flat, iron spatula-spoon. Salt. In the end the potatoes are almost in a cohered mass. If any pieces too big she cuts them as they cook with her iron implement.

She beats the eggs in a bowl, tips in the potatoes (slightly cooled; they have been transferred to a bowl) and mixes them well. The tortilla is cooked in an iron omelette pan with smoking oil. It puffs up. She holds a deep plate in her left hand and turns the tortilla into it. Then back into the pan. And process repeated (sometimes twice, it depends if she is satisfied with its appearance).

Enough for four to six people.

Notes:
1. For the initial cooking of the potatoes I still use a Spanish earthenware dish over direct heat, as did Juanita, although an ordinary frying pan serves perfectly well.
2. About that spatula-spoon: this is a characteristic Spanish kitchen implement, a round flat pusher, as it were, with a long handle, used mainly when the paella is cooking, and just right for moving the rice and other ingredients around in the pan. I use a thin wooden or metal icing spatula instead.
3. Really fresh eggs are necessary for a tortilla. Stale ones don't puff up, and so produce a flat omelette.

BAKED EGGS
œufs en cocotte

Have your little fireproof china dishes ready with a good lump of *butter* in each, and an *egg* for each person ready broken into separate saucers. Put the little dishes into the oven at 375°F and take them out as soon as the butter has melted, slide an egg into each, pour a large tablespoon of *heavy cream* onto the egg, avoiding the yolk, return them to the oven. They will take 4–5 minutes to cook, allowing perhaps ½ a minute less for those on the top shelf.

If you leave them too long, the yolks get hard and the dish is ruined, so be on the alert to see that they are taken out of the oven at the exact moment.

Experience and knowledge of the idiosyncrasies of one's own oven are the mediums of success here. No pepper or salt should be added, except at table, but a very little cut fresh tarragon when they come out of the oven is an acceptable addition.

POACHED EGGS

This is what Dr. Kitchiner, author of *The Cook's Oracle* (1829) has to say about poached eggs:

> The cook who wishes to display her skill in Poaching, must endeavour to procure Eggs that have been laid a couple of days, those that are quite newlaid are so milky that, take all the care you can, your cooking of them will seldom procure you the praise of being a Prime Poacher: You must have fresh Eggs, or it is equally impossible.
>
> The beauty of a Poached Egg is for the yolk to be seen blushing through the white—which should only be just sufficiently hardened, to form a transparent Veil for the Egg.
>
> My own method for poaching eggs I learnt from a cookery book published by the Buckinghamshire Women's Institute, and it has proved infallible.

First boil a saucepan of water, and into this dip each egg whole, in its shell, while you count about thirty, then take it out. When it comes to actually poaching the eggs, have a pan of fresh water boiling, add a teaspoon of vinegar, stir the water fast until a whirlpool has formed, and into this break the eggs, one at a time. 1–1½ minutes cooks them. Take them very carefully out with a perforated spoon. They will be rounded and the yolks covered with a "transparent Veil" instead of the ragged-looking affair which a poached egg too often turns out to be, and the alternative of the egg-poaching pan, which produces an over-cooked sort of egg-bun, is equally avoided.

It is interesting to note that Dr. Kitchiner instructs his readers to place poached eggs on bread "toasted on one side only." How right he is; I have never been able to understand the point of that sodden toast . . .

Try serving poached eggs on a piece of fresh, buttered bread; alternatively on a purée of some kind—split peas, corn or mushrooms, with pieces of fried bread around, but not under, the egg.

PIPÉRADE

Pipérade is the best known of all Basque dishes, and various recipes for it have appeared in English cookery books. It is a mixture of sweet peppers, tomatoes and onions, with eggs added at the end; the final result is a creamy scrambled-egg effect deliciously blended with the vegetables in which the sweet pepper flavor slightly dominates. Sometimes one meets it with the purée of onions, tomatoes and peppers topped with fried eggs, sometimes in the form of an omelette; the scrambled-egg version is the most characteristically Basque.

Pork fat or olive oil, 2 medium onions, 3 fairly large sweet red peppers or about 6 small green ones, in season in the Basque country long before the red ones, 1lb tomatoes, salt and pepper, marjoram, 6 eggs.

In a heavy frying or sauté pan melt some pork fat (sometimes olive oil is used for this dish, but pork, or even bacon fat, suits it better). Put in the sliced onions, and let them cook slowly, turning golden but not brown: then put in the peppers, cut into strips; let this cook until it is soft, then add the chopped tomatoes, with a seasoning of salt, ground black pepper and a little marjoram. Cook with the cover on the pan.

When the whole mixture has become almost the consistency of a purée, pour in the beaten eggs, and stir gently, exactly as for ordinary scrambled eggs. Take care not to let them get over-cooked.

With the pipérade are served slices of the famous Jambon de Bayonne, most of which is in fact made at Orthez, in the Béarn.

The Jambon de Bayonne is something like the Italian Prosciutto and imparts its particular flavor to many Basque and Béarnais *garbures* and daubes. Brochettes of calf's liver are sometimes served with the pipérade and a very good combination it is.

Enough for four people.

EGGS COOKED *with* TOMATOES *and* PEPPERS
chatchouka

This dish of eggs and vegetables is of Tunisian origin. It is made with a variety of vegetables—artichokes, fava beans, carrots, peas—according to the season. Chatchouka with tomatoes and peppers is a popular summer dish. Sometimes a little chopped or minced chicken or meat is cooked with the peppers, sometimes onions, and sometimes the chatchouka is cooked in individual earthenware egg dishes.

6 small green peppers, butter or olive oil, 8 tomatoes, salt and pepper, 4 eggs.

Remove the cores and seeds from the peppers, and cut them in strips. Heat a little oil or butter in a shallow earthenware dish. In this stew the peppers, and add the roughly chopped tomatoes, when the peppers are half cooked. Season with salt and pepper. When the tomatoes are soft, break in the eggs, whole, and cover the pan until they are cooked. Serve in the dish in which they have cooked.

Enough for four people.

QUICHE LORRAINE

As in all regional dishes of ancient origin which have eventually become national as well as purely local property, there have been various evolutions in the composition of a quiche. Also called, in different parts of the province, *galette*, *fiouse*, *tourte*, *flon* and *flan*, a quiche is a flat open tart, and originally it was made of bread dough just like the Provençal pissaladière and the Neapolitan pizza. Gradually the bread dough came to be replaced with pastry while the fillings, of course, vary enormously, from sweet purple quetsch or golden mirabelle plums to savory mixtures of onion, of chopped pork and veal, of cream flavored with poppy seeds, of cream and eggs and bacon, of cream and cream cheese. According to its filling the tart will be called a *quiche aux pruneaux*, *quiche à l'oignon*, and so on. The one universally known as the quiche Lorraine contains smoked bacon, cream and eggs. Parisian, and English, cooks often add Gruyère cheese, but Lorrainers will tell you that this is not the true quiche Lorraine, whose history goes back at least as far as the sixteenth century.

> For the pastry: *4 tablespoons chilled butter, ¾ cup all-purpose flour, sifted, salt, 1 egg, a little water.*

> For the filling: *6 thin slices bacon, 1¼ cups heavy cream, 3 egg yolks, 1 whole egg, pepper, salt.*

Cut the butter into little pieces and crumble it thoroughly with the sifted flour, adding a good pinch of salt. Break in the egg and mix the dough with your hands. Add enough water (1 to 2 teaspoons) to make the dough soft, but it should still be firm enough to come away clean from the bowl or board. Simply knead it into a ball, wrap it in waxed paper and chill it for a minimum of 2 hours. When the time comes to use it, roll it out very thin and line an 8-inch tart pan with it, and with a fork prick the surface.

Preheat the oven to 400°F. For the filling cut the bacon into 1-inch-wide strips. Cook them in a frying pan for a minute so that some of the fat runs. Arrange them in circles on the pastry. Have ready the cream mixed with the very well-beaten yolks of 3 eggs plus 1 whole egg, and well seasoned with freshly ground pepper and a little salt (taking into account the saltiness of the bacon). Pour this mixture over the bacon and transfer immediately to the preheated oven. Leave it for 20 minutes, then cook for another 10 minutes at a lowered temperature, 350°F. By this time the filling should be puffed up almost like a soufflé, and golden brown. Let it rest a minute or two after you take it from the oven, to make it easier to cut, but don't wait until it has fallen before serving it.

Enough for four people.

ONION TART

tarte à l'oignon

This is the famous Alsatian speciality. It makes a truly lovely first course.

> For the pastry: *¾ cup all-purpose flour, sifted, 4 tablespoons chilled butter, 1 egg, salt, water.*

> For the filling: *1½lb onions, butter and oil for cooking the onions, salt, nutmeg and plenty of freshly ground pepper, 3 egg yolks, ⅔ cup heavy cream.*

Make a well in the sifted flour, put the butter cut in small pieces, the egg and a good pinch of salt in the middle. Blend quickly and lightly but thoroughly, with the fingertips. Add a very little water, just enough to make the dough moist, but it should come cleanly away from the bowl or board. Place the ball of dough on a floured board and with the heel of your palm gradually stretch the dough out, bit by bit, until it is a flat but rather ragged-looking sheet. Gather it up again, and repeat the process. It should all be done lightly and expeditiously, and is extremely simple although it sounds complicated written down. Roll it into a ball, wrap it in waxed paper and leave it to rest in a refrigerator for a minimum of 2 hours, so that it loses all elasticity and will not shrink or lose its shape during the baking. This is one version of the *pâte brisée* or *pâte à foncer* used for most open tarts in French cookery. Without being as rich or as complicated as puff pastry, it is light and crisp. But those who already have a satisfactory method for tart and flan pastries may prefer to stick to their own. In spite of all the cooking rules, the making of pastry remains a very personal matter.

For the filling, peel and slice the onions as finely as possible, taking care to discard the fibrous parts at the root of the onions. Melt 4 tablespoons of butter and a little oil in a heavy frying pan. In this cook the onions, covered, until they are quite soft and pale golden. They must not fry, and they should be stirred from time to time to make sure they are not sticking. They will take about ½ an hour. Season with salt, nutmeg and pepper. Stir in the very well-beaten yolks and the cream, and leave until the time comes to cook the tart.

Oil an 8-inch tart pan. Roll out your pastry as thinly as possible (the great thing about this dish, as also the quiches of Lorraine, is that there should be a lot of creamy filling on very little pastry). Line the pan with the pastry, pressing it gently into position with your knuckle. Pour in the filling, cook in the center of a fairly hot oven, with the pan standing on a baking sheet, at 400°F, for 30 minutes. Serve very hot.

Enough for four to six people.

LEEK *and* CREAM PIE
flan de poireaux à la berrichonne

Under the name of flamiche or flamique a very similar dish is made in Picardy and other parts of northern France, but does not usually include the ham, more leeks (3lb) and less cream (⅔ cup) being used for the filling. Sometimes a bread dough or yeast pastry is used (in this case, reduce the amount of filling by one third, to allow for the rising of the pastry) and sometimes the *flamiche* is covered over with a lid of pastry so that it becomes more like a pasty.

Line an 8-inch pie tin with *pastry*, as for the Onion Tart on page 90 or the Quiche Lorraine, page 89. Chop the white part of 2lb of *leeks* and let them melt in *butter*. Add 2oz of lean *ham* cut into dice. Spread this mixture on the pastry.

Beat together 3 *egg yolks* and 1¼ cups *heavy cream*; season with *salt* and *pepper*. Pour this mixture over the leeks, put a few small pieces of *butter* on the top, and cook in a medium hot oven at 375°F for 30–40 minutes.

Enough for four people.

PASTA

ASCIUTTA

On the 15th of November 1930, at a banquet at the restaurant Penna d'Oca in Milan, the famous Italian futurist poet Marinetti launched his much publicized campaign against all established forms of cooking and, in particular, against pastasciutta. "Futurist cooking," said Marinetti, "will be liberated from the ancient obsession of weight and volume, and one of its principal aims will be the abolition of pastasciutta. Pastasciutta, however grateful to the palate, is an obsolete food; it is heavy, brutalizing, and gross; its nutritive qualities are deceptive; it induces scepticism, sloth, and pessimism."

The day after this diatribe was delivered the Italian press broke into an uproar; all classes participated in the dispute which ensued. Every time pastasciutta was served either in a restaurant or a private house interminable arguments arose. One of Marinetti's supporters declared that "our pastasciutta, like our rhetoric, suffices merely to fill the mouth." Doctors, asked their opinions, were characteristically cautious: "Habitual and exaggerated consumption of pastasciutta is definitely fattening." "Heavy consumers of pastasciutta have slow and placid characters; meat eaters are quick and aggressive." "A question of taste and of the cost of living. In any case, diet should be varied, and should never consist exclusively of one single element." The Duke of Bovino, Mayor of Naples, plunged into the fight with happy abandon. "The angels in Paradise," he affirmed to a reporter, "eat nothing but *vermicelli al pomodoro*." To which Marinetti replied that this confirmed his suspicions with regard to the monotony of Paradise and of the life led by the angels.

Marinetti and his friends proceeded to divert themselves and outrage the public with the invention and publication of preposterous new dishes. Most of these were founded on the shock principle of combining unsuitable and exotic ingredients (mortadella with nougat, pineapple with sardines, cooked salami immersed in a bath of hot black coffee flavored with eau-de-Cologne, an aphrodisiac drink composed of pineapple juice, eggs, cocoa, caviar, almond paste, red pepper, nutmeg, cloves and Strega). Meals were to be eaten to the accompaniment of perfumes (warmed, so that the bald-headed should not suffer from the cold), to be sprayed over the diners, who, fork in the right hand, would stroke meanwhile with the left some suitable substance—velvet, silk or emery paper.

Marinetti's bombshell contained a good deal of common sense; diet and methods of cookery must necessarily evolve at the same time as other habits and customs. But behind this amiable fooling lurked a sinister note: the fascist obsession with nationalism and patriotism, the war to come. "Spaghetti is no food for fighters." In the "conflict to come the victory will be to the swift." "Pastasciutta is antivirile . . . A weighty and encumbered stomach cannot be favorable to physical enthusiasm towards women." The costly import of foreign flour for pastasciutta should be stopped, to boost the national cultivation of rice. The snobbery of the Italian aristocracy and *haute bourgeoisie*, who had lost their heads over American customs, cocktail parties, foreign films, German music, and French food, was damned by Marinetti as *esterofil* (pro-foreign) and anti-Italian.

Marinetti's effort was not the first that had been made to reform the Italian diet. In the sixteenth century a Genoese doctor had denounced the abuse of pasta. Towards the end of the eighteenth century a campaign was instituted against the consumption of excessive quantities of macaroni. Innumerable volumes from the hands of eminent scientists and men of letters proved unavailing. Not only was the passion for pastasciutta too deeply rooted in the tastes of the people, but there was also a widely diffused superstition that macaroni was the antidote to all ills, the universal panacea.

Another effort was made in the first half of the nineteenth century by the scientist Michele Scropetta; he, again, achieved nothing concrete. Had it not been for the war Marinetti's campaign might have achieved a certain success; but however aware enlightened Italians may be of the unsuitability of pasta as a daily food, the fact remains that the majority of southern Italians (in the north it is replaced by rice or polenta) continue to eat pastasciutta at midday and probably some kind of *pasta in brodo* at night. Considering the cost of living, this is not surprising; freshly made pasta such as tagliatelle and fettuccine is cheap and versatile. According to circumstances it may be eaten economically with tomato sauce and cheese, with fresh tomatoes when they are cheap, with butter and cheese, with oil and garlic without cheese. The whole dish will cost rather less than two eggs, is immediately satisfying, and possesses the further advantage that every Italian could prepare a dish of spaghetti blindfold, standing on his head in his sleep.

from Italian Food, *1954*

PASTA

The different varieties of pasta are countless, and to add to the confusion each province has different names for almost identical kinds. There are two main distinctions to be made with regard to genuine Italian pasta. There is *pasta fatta in casa* (home-made pasta), and the kind which is mass-produced and dried in the factory and which will keep almost indefinitely.

When you see the words *pasta di pura semola di grano duro* printed on the label of a packet of spaghetti or other pasta, it means that the product is made from fine flour obtained from the cleaned endosperm or heart of the durum (hard) wheat grain; the cream of the wheat, in fact. What we know as semolina is produced in a similar way, but is more coarsely milled.

Some kinds of factory-produced pasta are made with eggs, some without. Pasta colored green with spinach is also sold in packets. The Italians have brought the manufacture of pasta to a fine art, and the difference between homemade and dried pasta is chiefly one of texture. Dried must, of course, be cooked for about 10 minutes, whereas freshly made pasta takes only about 5 minutes.

In Italy the amount of pasta allowed for each person is 3–4oz, whether homemade or dried. The latter is usually cooked in a large quantity of boiling salted water. It should be cooked *al dente*, that is, very slightly resistant, and it should be strained without delay. A warmed serving dish should be ready, and the pasta should be eaten as soon as it has been prepared.

An alternative, but little known, way of cooking manufactured pasta is to calculate 1 quart of water to every ¼lb of dried pasta. Bring the water to the boil; add a tablespoon of salt for every 2 quarts of water and add the pasta. After it comes back to the boil let it continue boiling for 3 minutes. Turn off the heat, cover the saucepan with a towel and the lid, leave it for 5–8 minutes according to the thickness of the pasta, e.g. 5 minutes for spaghettini, 8 for *maccheroni rigati,* which are short tubes, ridged and thick. At the end of this time the pasta should be just *al dente*.

I learned this excellent method from the directions given on a packet of Agnesi pasta bought in the early 1970s. I find it infinitely preferable to the old-fashioned way.

The addition of a generous lump of butter left to melt on the top of the pasta as it is served, or of a little olive oil put into the heated dish before the cooked pasta is turned into it, are both valuable improvements. Whether the sauce is served separately or stirred into the pasta is a matter of taste.

TAGLIATELLE *with* BOLOGNESE SAUCE
tagliatelle alla bolognese

Ragù is the true name of the Bolognese sauce which, in one form or another, has travelled round the world. In Bologna it is served mainly with *lasagne verdi*, but it can go with many other kinds of pasta. Fresh butter must be served as well, and plenty of grated Parmesan. This dish of pasta, known by name all over the world, is served in such a vast number of astounding ways, all of them incorrect (which would not matter if those ways happened to be successful), that it is a revelation to eat it cooked in the true Bolognese fashion. This is the recipe given me by Zia Nerina, a splendid woman, titanic of proportion but angelic of face and manner, who in the 1950s owned and ran the Trattoria Nerina in Bologna. Zia Nerina's cooking was renowned far beyond the confines of her native city.

> *3oz pancetta or prosciutto ("both fat and lean"), butter, 1 onion, 1 carrot, 1 small rib of celery, 8oz lean ground beef, 4oz chicken livers, 3 tablespoons tomato paste, ¾ cup dry white wine, salt and pepper, nutmeg, 1½ cups meat stock or water, 1 cup heavy cream or milk (optional), freshly grated Parmesan.*

Cut the pancetta or prosciutto into very small pieces and brown them gently in a small saucepan in about 1 tablespoon of butter. Add the onion, the carrot and the celery, all finely chopped. When they have browned, put in the raw ground beef, and then turn it over and over so that it all browns evenly. Now add the chopped chicken livers, and after 2 or 3 minutes the tomato paste, and then the white wine. Season with salt (having regard to the relative saltiness of the pancetta or prosciutto), pepper, and a scraping of nutmeg, and add the meat stock or water. Cover the pan and simmer the sauce very gently for 30–40 minutes. Some Bolognese cooks add at the last 1 cup of heavy cream or milk to the sauce, which makes it smoother. When the *ragù* is to be served with spaghetti or tagliatelle, mix it with the hot pasta in a heated dish so that the pasta is thoroughly impregnated with the sauce, and add a good piece of butter before serving. Hand the grated cheese separately.

Enough sauce for 1lb of pasta.

PENNE
with MASCARPONE

Mascarpone is a pure, double cream cheese made in northern Italy and sometimes eaten with sugar and strawberries in the same way as the French Crémets and Cœur à la Crème. It makes a most delicious sauce for pasta. The ordinary milk curd cheese (like mozzarella) can also be used for a pasta sauce, but the double cream variety produces a dish altogether more subtle.

One or other variety of small pasta such as little shells, pennine (small quills) and so on can equally be used for this dish; as can tagliatelle, the narrow ribbon noodles, usually called fettuccine in Rome. The green ones are particularly attractive for this dish because of the contrast of the green pasta with the cream sauce.

The sauce is prepared as follows: in a saucepan you can serve from, melt a lump of *butter* and ½–¾ cup *mascarpone*. It must just gently heat, not boil. Into this mixture put your cooked and drained *pasta*. Turn it round and round, adding 2 or 3 tablespoons of grated *Parmesan*. Add a dozen or so shelled and roughly chopped *walnuts*. Serve more grated cheese separately.

This is an exquisite dish when well prepared, but it is filling and rich, so a little goes a long way.

Enough sauce for 1lb of pasta.

FETTUCCINE
with FRESH TOMATO SAUCE
fettuccine alla marinara

Fettuccine are homemade ribbon noodles. The ready-made kind will, however, do just as well for this dish, which is Neapolitan.

Cook the *fettuccine* as usual; 5 minutes before they are ready make the sauce. Into a frying pan put a good covering of *olive oil*; into this when it is hot but not smoking throw at least 3 cloves of sliced *garlic*; let them cook half a minute. Add 6 or 7 ripe *tomatoes*, each cut in about 6 pieces; they are to cook for about 3 minutes only, the point of the sauce being that the tomatoes retain their natural flavor and are scarcely cooked, while the juice that comes out of them (they must, of course, be ripe tomatoes) amalgamates with the oil and will moisten the pasta. At the last moment stir in several leaves of fresh *basil*, simply torn into 2 or 3 pieces each, and season the sauce with *salt* and *pepper*. Pour the sauce on top of the fettuccine in the serving dish, and serve the grated *cheese* separately.

This sauce is also thoroughly to be recommended for all kinds of pasta, rice and dried vegetables such as white beans and chickpeas.

Enough sauce for 1lb of pasta.

MACARONI CARBONARA

A Roman dish, and a welcome change from the customary pasta with tomato sauce. It can be made with any shaped macaroni, spaghetti or noodles. Sometimes rigatoni (short, thick, ribbed macaroni) are used for this dish.

Cook the *pasta* in the usual way, in plenty of boiling salted water. Drain it and put it into a heated dish. Have ready 4oz *pancetta*, or *coppa* (Italian cured pork shoulder), cut into short matchstick lengths, and fried gently in *butter*. When the macaroni is ready in its dish add to the pancetta or coppa 2 beaten *eggs* and stir as you would for scrambled eggs, pouring the whole mixture onto the macaroni at the precise moment when the eggs are beginning to thicken, so that they present a slightly granulated appearance without being as thick as scrambled eggs. Give the whole a good stir with a wooden spoon so that the egg and ham mixture is evenly distributed, add some grated *Parmesan*, and serve more Parmesan separately.

Enough sauce for 12oz of pasta.

SPAGHETTI *with* CLAMS
spaghetti alle vongole

One of the regular dishes of Roman restaurants as well as of Naples and the southern coast. Vongole are very small clams. If you can't get hold of them, use mussels or other small clams instead.

> *4 dozen littleneck clams or mussels if they are in their shells (½lb if they are already cooked and shelled), olive oil, an onion, 2 or 3 cloves of garlic, tomatoes, parsley.*

Clean the shellfish carefully, scrubbing them first and leaving them under cold running water until all the grit and sand have disappeared. Put them into a pan over a fairly fast flame and let the shells open. Drain them. Remove the shells. In a little warmed olive oil, sauté a chopped onion and 2 or 3 cloves of garlic (more if you like). Add 1½lb of chopped and skinned ripe tomatoes (or the contents of 14oz tin of Italian peeled tomatoes), and when this has been reduced somewhat, add the clams or mussels and a handful of chopped parsley. As soon as the shellfish are hot the sauce is ready. Pour it over the cooked spaghetti in the dish.

Cheese is never served with *spaghetti alle vongole*.

Enough sauce for 1lb of pasta.

SPAGHETTI
with OIL and GARLIC
spaghetti all'olio e aglio

Pasta is often eaten in Italy with no embellishment but oil and garlic. Those who are particularly addicted to spaghetti and to garlic will find this dish excellent, others will probably abominate it. It is essential that the oil be olive oil and of good quality.

When your *spaghetti* (about 1lb) is cooked, barely warm a cup of *oil* in a small pan, and into it stir whatever quantity of finely chopped *garlic* you fancy. Let it soak in the oil a bare minute, without frying, then stir the whole mixture into the spaghetti. You can add chopped *parsley* or any other herb, and of course grated *cheese* if you wish, although the Neapolitans do not serve cheese with spaghetti cooked in this way. If you like the taste of garlic without wishing actually to eat the bulb itself, pour the oil onto the spaghetti through a strainer, leaving the chopped garlic behind.

Enough for four to six people.

SPAGHETTI with OIL, GARLIC and CHILE
spaghetti all'olio, aglio e saetini

Cook the *spaghetti* in the usual way, put it into a hot dish, and pour over it a generous amount of very hot *olive oil* in which have been fried several coarsely chopped cloves of *garlic* and some *hot red pepper flakes*.

Enough sauce for 1lb of pasta.

TRENETTE *with* PESTO

This is perhaps the best pasta dish in the whole of Italy. Trenette are the Genoese version of fine pasta, about the thickness of a match, and the same shape, but in long pieces. The pasta is cooked as usual, and when it is ready in the serving dish, about 2 tablespoonfuls of pesto (which is neither cooked nor heated) are heaped up on the top, and on top of the pesto a large piece of butter. The butter and the sauce are mixed into the pasta at the table. Grated Parmesan or Pecorino is served separately. Spaghetti, lasagne, tagliatelle, in fact any pasta you fancy, can be served with pesto.

This sauce is eaten by the Genoese with all kinds of pasta, with gnocchi and as a flavoring for soups. The Genoese claim that their basil has a far superior flavor to that grown in any other part of Italy, and assert that a good pesto can only be made with Genoese basil. As made in Genoa it is certainly one of the best sauces yet invented for pasta and 1 tablespoon of pesto stirred in at the last minute gives a most delicious flavor to a minestrone. Try it also with baked potatoes instead of butter.

> *1 large bunch of fresh basil, garlic, salt, 2 tablespoons each of pine nuts and grated Sardo or Parmesan cheese, ¼–⅓ cup olive oil.*

Pound the basil leaves (there should be about 1 packed cup when the stalks have been removed) in a mortar with 1 or 2 cloves of garlic, a little salt and the pine nuts. Add the cheese. (Sardo cheese is the pungent Sardinian ewe's milk cheese which is exported in large quantities to Genoa to make pesto. Parmesan and Sardo are sometimes used in equal quantities, or all Parmesan, which gives the pesto a milder flavor.)

When the pesto is a thick purée start adding the olive oil, a little at a time. Stir it steadily and see that it is amalgamating with the other ingredients, as the finished sauce should have the consistency of a creamed butter. If made in larger quantities pesto may be stored in jars, covered with a layer of olive oil.

Enough sauce for 1lb of pasta.

GREEN GNOCCHI

gnocchi verdi

This quantity is sufficient for four people for a first course. If they are to be the mainstay of a meal make the quantities half as much again; but as the cooking of these gnocchi is an unfamiliar process to most people, it is advisable to try out the dish with not more than the quantities given.

> *1lb spinach, salt, pepper, nutmeg, a little butter, 1 cup ricotta, 2 eggs,*
> *3 tablespoons of flour, ⅓ cup (1½oz) grated Parmesan cheese, and for the*
> *sauce plenty of melted butter and grated Parmesan cheese.*

Cook the cleaned spinach with a little salt but no water. Drain it, press it absolutely dry, then chop it finely. Put it into a pan with salt, pepper, nutmeg, a nut of butter and the mashed ricotta. Stir all the ingredients together over a low flame for 5 minutes. Remove the pan from the fire and beat in the eggs, the flour and the grated Parmesan. Leave the mixture in the refrigerator for several hours, or, better, overnight.

Spread a pastry board with flour, form little croquettes about the size of a cork with the spinach mixture, roll them in the flour, and when they are all ready drop them carefully into a large pan of barely simmering, slightly salted water.

(Do not be alarmed if the mixture seems rather soft; the eggs and the flour hold the gnocchi together as soon as they are put into the boiling water.)

Either the gnocchi must be cooked in a very large saucepan or else the operation must be carried out in two or three relays, as there must be plenty of room for them in the pan. When they rise to the top, which will be in 5–8 minutes, they are ready. They will disintegrate if left too long. Take them out with a perforated spoon, drain them carefully in a colander or sieve, and when the first batch is ready slide them into a shallow ovenproof dish already prepared with 2 tablespoons of melted butter and a thin layer of grated Parmesan cheese. Put the dish in a low (200°F) oven to keep hot while the rest of the gnocchi are cooked. When all are done, put another 2 tablespoons of butter and a generous amount of cheese over them and leave the dish in the oven for 5 minutes.

The
MARKETS
of FRANCE:
Cavaillon

It is a Sunday evening in mid-June. The cafés of Cavaillon are crammed. There isn't an inch to park your car. The noise is tremendous. In the most possible of the hotels—it goes by the name of Toppin—all the rooms are taken by seven o'clock. But the little Auberge La Provençale in the rue Chabran is quite quiet and you can enjoy a good little dinner—nothing spectacular, but genuine and decently cooked food well served—and go to bed early. The chances are you won't sleep much though, because Monday is the big market day in Cavaillon and soon after midnight the carts and lorries and vans of the big fruit farmers' cooperatives, of the market gardeners, of the tomato and garlic and onion growers, will start rattling and roaring and rumbling into the great open market in the place du Clos.

At dawn they will be unloading their melons and asparagus, their strawberries and red currants and cherries, their apricots and peaches and pears and plums, their green almonds, beans, lettuces, shining new white onions, new potatoes, vast bunches of garlic. By six o'clock the ground will be covered with *cageots*, the chip vegetable and fruit baskets, making a sea of soft colors and shadowy shapes in the dawn light. The air of the place is filled with the musky scent of those little early Cavaillon melons, and then you become aware of another powerfully conflicting smell— rich, clove-like, spicy. It is the scent of sweet basil, and it is coming from the far end of the market where a solitary wrinkled old man sits on an upturned basket, scores and scores of basil plants ringed all around him like a protective hedge. With a beady eye he watches the drama of the market place. The dealers, exporters and wholesalers walking round inspecting the produce, discussing prices, negotiating; the hangers-on standing about in groups smoking, chatting; the market police and official inspectors strolling round seeing that all is in order.

On the whole the scene is quiet, quieter at least than you would expect, considering that this is one of the most important wholesale fruit and vegetable markets in France, the great distributing center for the *primeurs* of the astonishingly fertile and productive areas of the Vaucluse and the

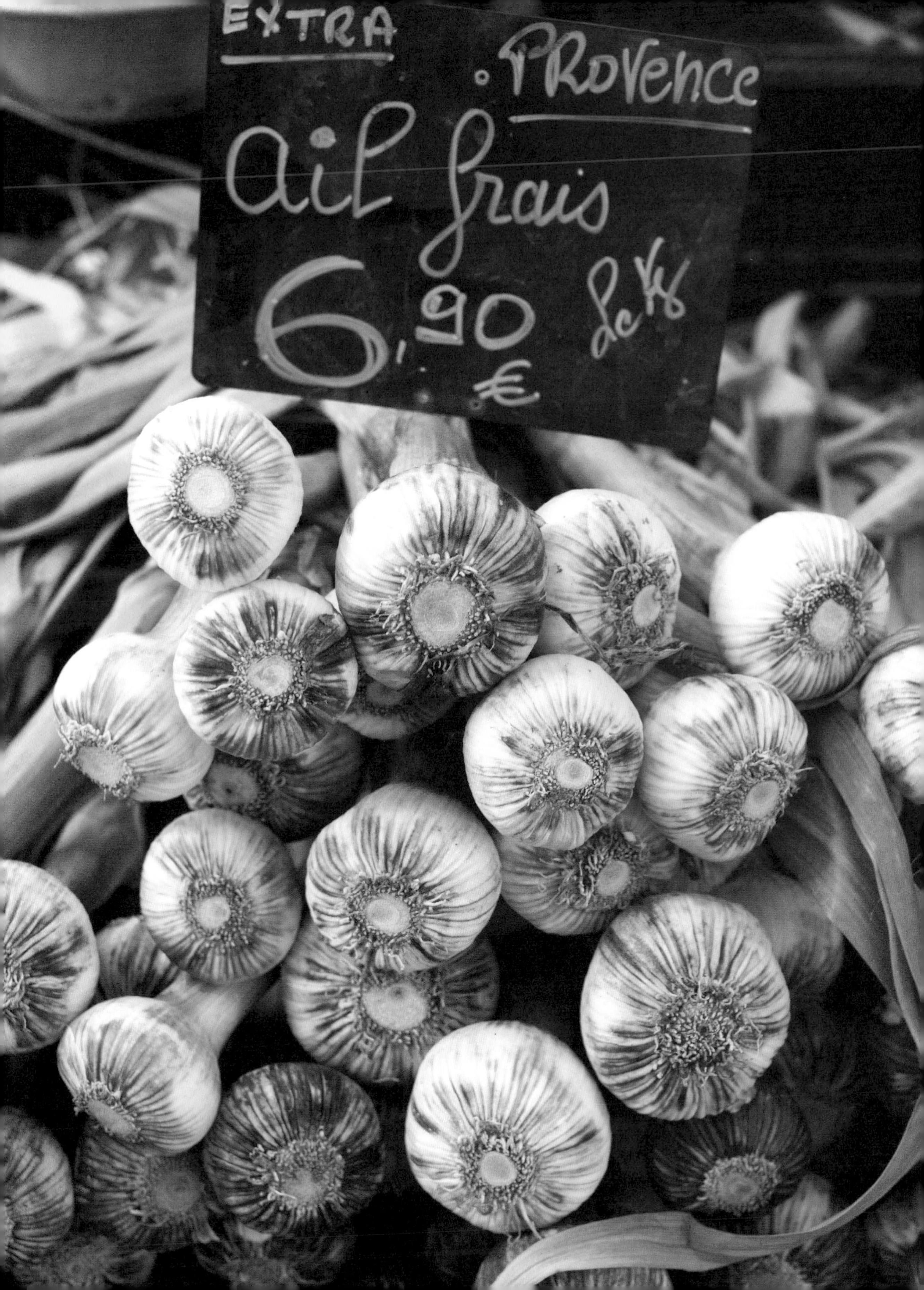
EXTRA
PROVENCE
ail frais
6,90 €
le kg

Comtat Venaissin—areas which less than a hundred years ago were desperately poor, inadequately irrigated, isolated for lack of roads and transport, earthquake-stricken, devastated by blights which destroyed the cereal crops and the vines.

It was with the building of the railways connecting Provence with Paris and the north, with Marseille and the ports of the Mediterranean to the south, that the possibilities of the Rhône and Durance valleys for intensive fruit and vegetable cultivation first began to be understood. New methods of irrigation, the planting of fruit trees in large areas where the vines had been stricken, the division of the land into small fields broken with tall cypress hedges as windbreaks against the scourging mistral, the ever-increasing demand in Paris and the big towns of the north for early vegetables, and the tremendous industry of these Provençal cultivators have done the rest. And to such effect that last year eighty thousand kilos (176,000lbs) of asparagus came into Cavaillon market alone between 15 April and 15 May; in the peak month of July three hundred tons of melons daily; five hundred tons of tomatoes every day in July and August. Altogether some hundred and sixty thousand tons of vegetables and fruit leave Cavaillon every year, about fifty per cent by rail, the rest by road. And Cavaillon, although the most important, is by no means the only big market center in the neighborhood. Avignon, Châteaurenard, Bolléne, Pertuis, all dispatch their produce by special trains to the north; vast quantities of fruit are absorbed locally by the jam and fruit-preserving industries of Apt and Carpentras; and every little town and village has its own retail vegetable and fruit market, every day in the bigger towns, once or twice a week in less populated places.

But now seven o'clock strikes in the market at Cavaillon. The lull is over. This is the moment when the goods change hands. Pandemonium breaks loose. The dealers snatch the baskets of produce they have bought and rush them to waiting lorries. A cartload of garlic vanishes from under your nose. A mountain of melons evaporates in a wink. If you try to speak to anybody you will be ignored, if you get in the way you'll be knocked down in the wild scramble to get goods away to Paris, London, Brussels and all the great centers of northern and eastern France. Suddenly, the market place is deserted.

At eight o'clock you emerge from the café where you have had your breakfast coffee and croissant. The market place is, to put it mildly, astir once more. It is surrounded by vans and lorries disgorging cheap dresses and overalls, plastic kitchenware, shoes and scarves and bales of cotton, piles of plates and jugs, nails and screws and knives, farm implements and packets of seeds, cartons of dried-up-looking biscuits and trays of chemically colored sweets.

You dive down a side street where you have spied a festoon of pretty cotton squares, and there, under gaudy painted colonnades, lilac and orange, cinnamon and lemon and rose, in patterns more typical of Marseille or the Levant than of Cavaillon, the retail market stalls are already doing business. The displays seem rather tame after the wholesale market and there is not a melon to be seen. It is too early in the season, they are still too expensive for the housewives of Cavaillon. Five thousand francs a kilo they were fetching today, and a week later in London shops 12s. 6d. each for little tiny ones. But the street opposite the painted colonnades leads into the square where more and more food stalls are opening and the housewives are already busy marketing. Here you can buy everything for a picnic lunch. Beautiful sprawling ripe tomatoes, a Banon cheese wrapped in chestnut leaves, Arles sausages, pâté, black olives, butter cut from a towering monolith, apricots, cherries.

It is still early and you can drive out towards Apt and branch off across the Lubéron. The roads are sinuous but almost empty, and they will take you through some of the most beautiful country in Provence. Perched on the hillsides are typical old Provençal villages, some, like Oppède-le-Vieux, crumbling, haunted, half-deserted, others like Bonnieux with a flourishing modern village built below the old one, and up beyond Apt, through the dramatic stretch of ochre-mining country, the strange red-gold village of Roussillon appears to be toppling precariously on the edge of a craggy cliff. Round about here, the network of caves under the ochreous rocks has been turned into vast *champignonnières*, and at the modest little Restaurant David (no relation) you can eat the local cultivated mushrooms cooked *à la crème* or *à la provençale* with, naturally, olive oil, parsley and garlic. And the Rose d'Or, a little hotel opened only a few weeks ago, promises a welcome alternative to the establishments of Apt, Aix and Cavaillon.

from Vogue, *1960*

VEGETABLES

What, I am sometimes asked, is the difference between fresh and frozen vegetables; surely they are exactly the same? Astonishing though such a question may seem to anyone who knows what is really meant by fresh vegetables, I think the explanation is that to a great many English people vegetables mean simply an accompaniment to meat. Gravy and horseradish, mustard and mint, to say nothing of the meat itself, distract attention from second-rate or inadequately cooked vegetables. Eaten for themselves alone, as a separate dish, vegetables take on a very different significance. Both their charms and their defects become more apparent. Apart from cauliflower cheese, we haven't much tradition in the way of vegetable dishes which stand on their own. But we have plenty of vegetables, and often it is the commonplace ones like onions and beets, carrots and spinach and leeks which make the most delicious dishes.

It is in the matter of vegetables and fruit that a country's eating habits evolve most rapidly. There was a time, after all, when there were no potatoes in England, when the tomato was new to Italy, when petits pois were first brought to France (and caused a furor at the court of Louis XIV), when bananas, grapefruit and the cultivated mushrooms we now take for granted were exciting novelties. Not so long ago, French beans meant only coarse scarlet runners, but now we can buy several varieties of string beans and dwarf beans. Eggplants, sweet peppers and avocados have become commonplace in our shops. Enterprising English growers are supplying us with little zucchini as an alternative to gigantic summer squash.

So, I wonder if, eventually, we shall not come round to the habit, taken for granted in French cookery, of regarding vegetable dishes as an important part of the meal rather than simply as an adjunct to the roast. If we do, we shall surely find that we enjoy the meat course more as well as the vegetables, for both must, when required to stand on their own, be more carefully bought and more meticulously cooked.

VENETIAN ARTICHOKES

carciofi alla veneziana

Globe artichokes are almost one of the staple vegetables of Italy. There are several different varieties and they are cooked in a good many different ways. The large green ones, which are so tender that the whole vegetable can be eaten, are at their best in the famous Roman dish *carciofi alla Giudea* (fried whole in oil), or *alla Romana*, stewed in oil and garlic. They can be cut into slices and fried, sometimes in batter, and served as part of a *fritto misto*. Very tiny artichokes are preserved in oil. The medium-sized ones with violet-colored leaves are perfectly delicious stewed in oil and white wine, and equally good cut in papery slices and either cooked in butter as an accompaniment to veal or served raw with a seasoning of oil and lemon. Hearts of artichokes are often combined with eggs in a frittata, also in a kind of omelette cooked in the oven, and are an important ingredient of the excellent *torta pasqualina*, Genoese Easter pie.

In some parts of Italy artichoke hearts are sold ready prepared for cooking. You take off the outside leaves and with a sharp knife cut off two thirds of the top of the artichoke. Take out the choke and trim round the outside so that only the heart and a few of the inside leaves are left. As each one is ready throw it into cold water in which you have squeezed lemon juice.

For this dish the small dark violet-leaved **artichokes** are used. Put 6 or 8 of them, with only the outer leaves cut away, into a braising pan, covered with equal parts of **olive oil**, **white wine** and water. Stew them gently, with the cover on the pan, for an hour, then take off the lid, turn up the flame, and let the liquid reduce until only the oil is left.

Enough for three to four people.

TURKISH EGGPLANTS
aubergines à la turque

Eggplants are particularly successful when mixed with tomatoes in some form or other and they also make interesting purées and salads, the kind of little dishes which are served either as an hors d'œuvre or with meat, like a chutney (see recipe on page 31). Eggplants are best cooked in olive oil rather than in butter or dripping; they always have a warm southern look about them, especially when they are cooked with their purple skins on. Most eggplant dishes are as good cold as they are hot, and they can also be heated up without deteriorating in any way, so they are a most versatile vegetable.

> *2 large eggplants (the round variety are best for this dish), salt, olive oil,*
> *3 large onions, ½lb tomatoes, garlic, ground allspice, sugar.*

Cut the unpeeled eggplants into thick, round slices. Salt them and leave them to drain in a colander for an hour or two. Fry them in oil so that they are browned on both sides. Take them out of the pan and fry the thinly sliced onions, not crisply, but just golden yellow, then add the skinned and chopped tomatoes, and a clove or two of crushed garlic. Season with salt, a teaspoon of the allspice, and a little sugar. Cook until you have a thick sauce. Arrange the eggplant slices in an oiled baking dish, put a tablespoonful of the sauce on each slice of eggplant, and bake in a moderate oven (350°F) for 40–50 minutes. Can be served hot but best cold.

Enough for four people.

PROVENÇAL EGGPLANT MOUSSE

papeton d'aubergines

The story goes that one of the Avignon Popes complained that Provençal cooking was not as good as that of Rome, and his cook invented this recipe in order to prove that he was wrong. It is also recounted that the first *papeton* was presented to the Pope in the form of a mitre.

6 eggplants (the small round or oblong varieties), salt, olive oil, ground pepper, a clove of garlic, milk, 3 eggs.

Peel the eggplants, cut them in thick slices, salt them and leave them to drain. Stew them in olive oil in a covered pan, so that they remain moist; drain them and chop or mash them. Season and add a chopped clove of garlic, ¾ cup of milk and 3 eggs. Turn into a lightly oiled mold. Cook for 25 minutes in a bain-marie. Turn out and serve covered with a thick fresh tomato sauce flavored with fresh basil (page 305).

Instead of being turned out, the *papeton* can be served in the dish in which it has cooked, with the sauce poured on the top, or offered separately. A much easier system.

Enough for four people.

FAVA BEANS *with* BACON

Melt 2oz of diced *pancetta* (or prosciutto, or cold pork) in a little *butter*. Add 2 cups of shelled, cooked and peeled *fava beans*, 2 or 3 tablespoons of light *béchamel sauce* (see page 298), a little *heavy cream*, a very little chopped *parsley*. Simmer together for 5 minutes.

Enough for four to five people.

FAVA BEANS *with* YOGURT

A Middle Eastern dish, called *fistuqia*.

> *1½ cups fava beans, 2 tablespoons rice, a clove of garlic, ½ cup yogurt, salt and pepper, 1 egg.*

Boil the fava beans and the rice separately, drain them, peel the beans, and mix them together while hot. Stir the pounded garlic into the yogurt, season with salt and pepper and add the mixture to the beans and rice. Heat gently, then stir in the beaten egg. As soon as the sauce has thickened slightly, it is ready. Can be eaten hot or cold.

Enough for four people.

FAVA BEANS *with* EGG *and* LEMON

Cook 2 cups *fava beans* in boiling salted water. When they are ready drain and peel them, reserving about ½ cup of the water in which they have cooked. Add this to 2 *egg yolks* and the juice of a *lemon*. Heat over a very gentle flame, whisking all the time until the sauce is frothy and slightly thickened. Pour over the beans. Serve hot or cold.

Cooked artichoke hearts mixed with the beans are a good combination, and for an hors d'œuvre add a few large shrimp.

Enough for four to five people.

SLOW-COOKED BEANS
fasœil al fùrn

A Piedmontese country dish which is made with dried red borlotti beans, cooked all night in a slow oven and eaten the following day at lunch time. The Piedmontese custom is to put the dish to cook on Saturday night so that it is ready to take out of the oven when the family returns from Mass on Sunday at midday.

Put 1lb of *dried borlotti beans* (use dried white cannellini beans if borlotti are unobtainable) to soak in cold water for 12 hours. Chop a good quantity of *parsley* with several cloves of *garlic*, and add *pepper*, *cinnamon*, ground *cloves* and *mace*. Spread this mixture onto wide strips of *pork rind or pancetta*, roll them up, put them at the bottom of a deep earthenware bean pot, cover them with the beans, and add enough water to cover the beans by about 2 inches. Put the cover on the pot, and cook in a very slow oven (about 250°F), regulating the heat according to the time at which the beans are to be eaten. The slower they cook, the better the dish. Serve in soup plates as a very substantial midday meal. A splendid dish when you are busy, hard up, and have hungry people to feed.

Enough for six to eight people.

STEWED WHITE BEANS
fasoūlia

The Greek name for haricot beans. People who appreciate the taste of genuine olive oil in their food will like this dish.

Soak ½lb of *dried white (cannellini) beans* for 12 hours. Heat about ¼ cup of *olive oil* in a deep pan; put in the drained beans; lower the heat; stir the beans and let them simmer gently for 10 minutes, adding 2 cloves of *garlic*, a *bay leaf*, a branch of *thyme*, and 2 teaspoons of *tomato paste*. Add boiling water to cover the beans by about 1 inch. Cook them over a moderate heat for 3 hours. The liquid should have reduced sufficiently to form a thickish sauce. Squeeze in the juice of a *lemon*, add some *raw onion* cut into rings, some *salt* and *black pepper*, and leave them to cool.

Enough for four people.

GLAZED CARROTS

carottes vichy

This is one of the best-known vegetable dishes of French cookery. It is exceedingly simple, and makes a particularly welcome dish in the spring before the new peas and beans have arrived.

The water of the Vichy region is nonchalky and is therefore said to be particularly satisfactory for the cooking of vegetables, and it is this circumstance which no doubt gives the dish its name. A pinch of bicarbonate of soda (baking soda) in the water helps to produce the same effect. *Carottes Vichy* can be served as a garnish to meat or as a separate dish.

New **carrots** are scraped, and sliced into bias-cut rounds about ¼-inch thick. Put them into a heavy pan with 2 tablespoons of *butter*, a pinch of *salt*, 2 lumps (or 1½ teaspoons) of *sugar*, and 1 cup of water per 1lb of carrots. Cook uncovered for 20 to 25 minutes until nearly all the water has evaporated and the carrots are tender. Add another lump of butter and shake the pan so that the carrots do not stick. Add a little finely chopped *parsley* before serving.

Older carrots cut in quarters or chunks can be cooked in the same way but need a larger proportion of water. Add a teaspoon of sugar with the final lump of butter, and let this mixture cook until it has formed a thick syrup which coats the carrots, but don't let it turn to toffee.

Enough for four people.

PROVENÇAL LEEKS
poireaux à la provençale

> *3lb leeks (dark green, tops cut off), 2 tablespoons olive oil, salt and pepper,*
> *½lb tomatoes, 12 black olives, juice of 1 lemon, 2 teaspoons finely chopped*
> *lemon zest.*

Chop the cleaned leeks into 1½-inch lengths. Into a shallow heatproof dish put the oil and when it is warm, but not smoking, put in the leeks, add a little salt and pepper, cover the dish and simmer for 10 minutes. Add the tomatoes cut in halves, the pitted olives, the lemon juice and the chopped lemon zest and cook slowly for another 10 minutes. Serve in the dish in which it has been cooked. This is excellent cold as a salad.

Enough for four people.

ENDIVES BRAISED
in BUTTER
endives au beurre

Allow 1½ to 2 *endives* per person. Peel off any brown outside leaves; wipe the endives with a cloth. With a stainless knife cut each into ½-inch lengths. Melt a good lump of *butter* in a frying pan. Put in the vegetables; let them cook a few seconds, turning them about with a wooden spoon, before adding *salt*, turning down the heat and covering the pan. By this method they will be sufficiently cooked in about 10 minutes (as opposed to over an hour when they are cooked whole) but uncover them and shake the pan from time to time to make sure the endives are not sticking. Before serving add a squeeze of *lemon juice*.

A variation is to add a few little cubes of *pancetta or prosciutto*. Leeks are excellent prepared and cooked in the same way.

TOMATOES BAKED
with GRUYÈRE
tomates fromagées

Choose *medium-sized tomatoes*, cut off the tops, scoop out the flesh, sprinkle them with *salt*, turn them upside down and leave them to drain.

In a double boiler melt some *Gruyère cheese* with black *pepper*, *cayenne*, a little *Dijon mustard*, a drop of *white wine* and a pounded clove of *garlic*.

Fill the tomatoes with the mixture, which should be about the consistency of a Welsh rarebit. Bake for 10 minutes in the oven (375°F) and finish under the broiler.

ARMENIAN MUSHROOMS
champignons à l'arménienne

Mushrooms cooked in this way can be served as a separate course, as a garnish for scrambled eggs or omelettes, or eaten cold as a starter.

> *½lb mushrooms, olive oil, garlic, 2 slices of bacon, a glass of wine (red or white), parsley.*

Slice the mushrooms, sauté them in 2 tablespoons of olive oil; add a few very fine slivers of garlic, and the bacon cut in squares.

Let this cook a few minutes before pouring in a glass of wine, then cook fiercely for just 1 minute (to reduce the wine), turn the heat down, add the chopped parsley and simmer for 5 more minutes.

Enough for four people.

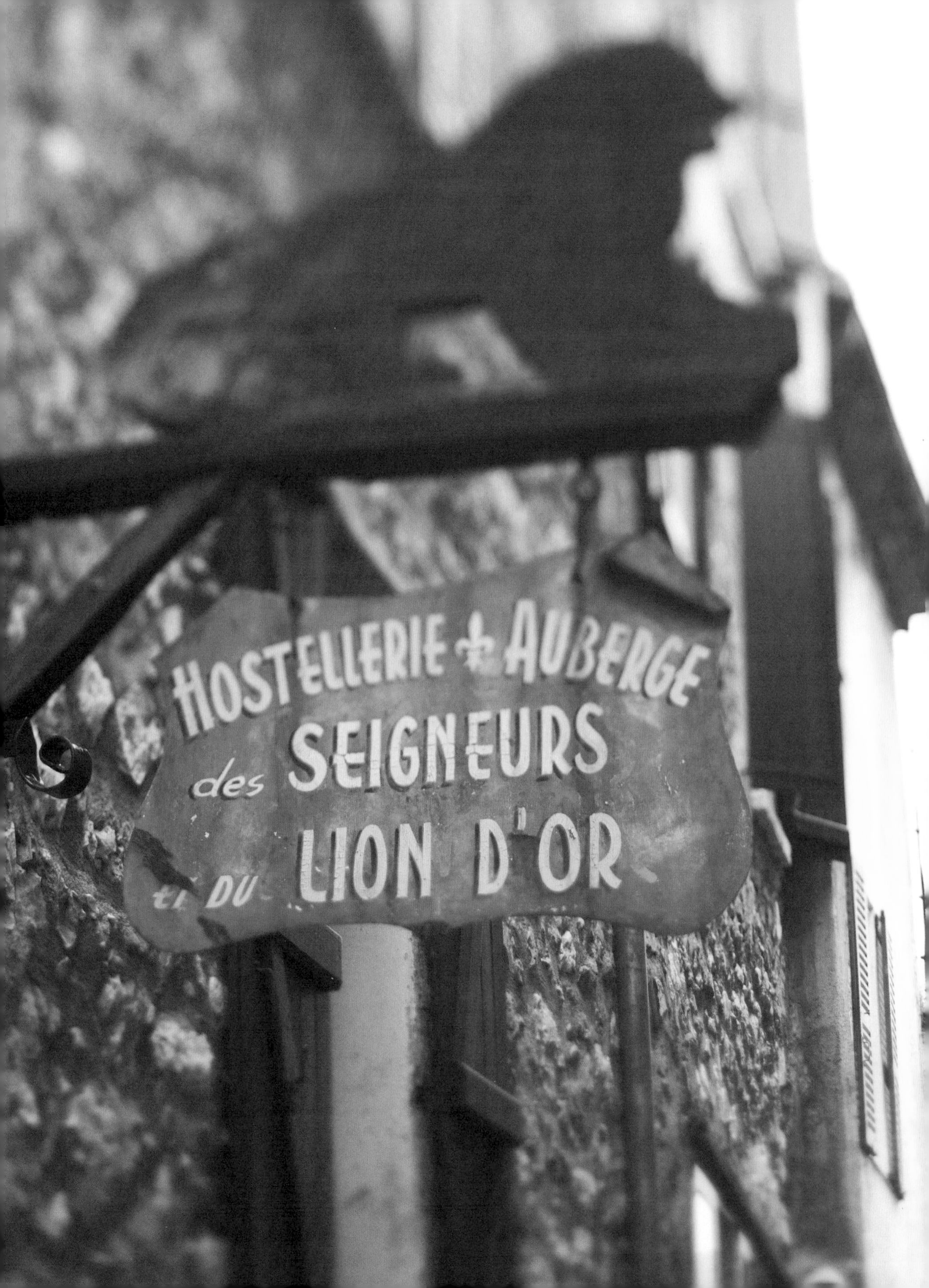
HOSTELLERIE AUBERGE
des SEIGNEURS
DU LION D'OR

SWEET PEPPER and TOMATO STEW

peperonata

A large onion, olive oil, butter, 8 red peppers, salt, 10 good ripe tomatoes.

Brown the sliced onion very lightly in a mixture of olive oil and butter. Add the peppers, cleaned, the seeds removed, and cut into strips; season them with salt. Simmer them for about 15 minutes, with the cover on the pan. Now add the tomatoes, peeled and quartered, and cook another 30 minutes. There should not be too much oil, as the tomatoes provide enough liquid to cook the peppers, and the resulting mixture should be fairly dry. Garlic can be added if you like.

To store for a few days in the refrigerator, pack the *peperonata* in a jar, and float enough olive oil on the top to seal the contents. Enough for six or seven people, but peperonata is so good when reheated that it is worth making a large amount at one time.

GREEN PEAS and HAM

piselli al prosciutto

The green peas which grow round about Rome are the most delicious I have ever tasted anywhere. Small, sweet, tender, and very green, they are really best simply stewed in butter. Cooked in this way they make a most delicate sauce for finely cut homemade pasta, or for *riso in bianco*. The Romans adore these green peas cooked with ham. Try this method with young English green peas before they become wrinkled and floury.

A small onion, butter, 2lb peas in the pod (or 2 cups shelled peas),
3oz prosciutto, cut into strips.

Melt the chopped onion in the butter, and let it cook very gently, so that it softens without browning. Put in the shelled peas and a very little water. After 5 minutes add the ham. In another 5–10 minutes the peas should be ready.

Enough for four people.

PÉRIGORD POTATOES
pommes de terre à l'échirlète

This is a way of cooking potatoes from the Périgord district, first class with grilled steak or roast game or by themselves.

Cook whole fairly small *potatoes*, in just enough water or, better still, *stock*, to cover them, adding 2 cloves of *garlic*; cover the pan. By the time the liquid is absorbed they should be cooked. Now put them in a pan with a tablespoon of *goose or pork fat* and the garlic and cook them slowly until they are brown all over. Turn them over two or three times.

Large potatoes cut in halves or quarters can also be successfully cooked by this excellent method.

1lb potatoes are enough for four to five people.

POTATOES COOKED
in MILK
pommes de terre au lait

This recipe demonstrates a method which turns old potatoes into something special, and makes new ones, as the French say, *extra*. For each 1lb of peeled and thickly sliced old *potatoes* or of small whole new ones, allow 2¼ cups of *milk*. Pour the cold uncooked milk over the potatoes in a saucepan, add a very little *salt*, simmer (if you let them gallop, the milk will boil over and the potatoes will stick, so look out), until the potatoes are just tender but not breaking up. Strain off the milk—it makes good vegetable soup stock—transfer the potatoes to a shallow ovenproof dish, sprinkle them very lightly with grated *nutmeg* and a little *thyme or basil*, add 3 or 4 tablespoons of the milk, and leave them uncovered in a low or moderate oven (325° to 350°F) for about 15 minutes.

Delicious with a plain roast, with steak, chicken, or just by themselves.

1lb potatoes are enough for four to five people.

GRATIN *of* POTATOES *and* CREAM

gratin dauphinois

Gratin dauphinois is a rich and filling regional dish from the Dauphiné. Some recipes include cheese and eggs, making it very similar to a *gratin savoyard*: but other regional authorities declare that the authentic *gratin dauphinois* is made only with potatoes and thick fresh cream. I give the second version, which is, I think, the better one; it is also the easier. And if it seems to the thrifty-minded outrageously extravagant to use a generous cup of cream to one pound of potatoes, I can only say that to me it seems a more satisfactory way of enjoying cream than pouring it over canned peaches or chocolate mousse.

It is not easy to say how many people this will serve; two, or three, or four, according to their capacity, and what there is to follow. Much depends also upon the quality of the potatoes used. Firm waxy varieties such as the fingerling or Yukon Gold make a gratin lighter and also more authentic than that made with routine commercial russets or Burbanks which are in every respect second best.

Two more points concerning the proportions of a *gratin dauphinois*: as the quantity of potatoes is increased the proportion of cream may be slightly diminished. Thus, for 3lb of potatoes, 3¼ cups of cream will be amply sufficient; and the choice of cooking dish is also important, for the potatoes and cream should, always, fill the dish to within approximately ¾ inch of the top.

Peel 1lb of waxy yellow *potatoes*, and slice them in even rounds no thicker than a penny; this operation is very easy with the aid of a mandoline. Rinse them thoroughly in cold water—this is most important—then shake them dry in a cloth. Put them in layers in a shallow earthenware dish which has been rubbed with *garlic* and well buttered. Season with *pepper* and *salt*. Pour 1¼ cups of thick *heavy cream* over them; strew with little pieces of butter; cook them for 1½ hours in a low oven, 300°F. During the last 10 minutes turn the oven up fairly high (about 400°F) to get a fine golden crust on the potatoes. Serve in the dish in which they have cooked.

The best way, in my view, of appreciating the charm of a *gratin dauphinois* is to present the dish entirely on its own, as a first course to precede grilled or plain roast meat or poultry, or a cold roast to be eaten with a simple green salad.

POTATOES *in* PARCHMENT

pommes de terre en papillote

Nicolas Soyer, grandson of the famous Alexis, spent years perfecting the system of paper-bag cookery and in 1911 published a book extolling its advantages. Indeed they are many. I can vouch for the excellence of this method for new potatoes.

Preheat the oven to 375°F. Scrape 24 very small **new potatoes**. Put them on a fair-sized square of parchment paper, with 2 leaves of **mint**, a little **salt** and 4 tablespoons of **butter**. Fold the paper over diagonally into a triangle, and then fold down the two edges so that the "bag" is completely sealed. Put it on a baking sheet into the preheated oven, and cook for about 35 minutes. They will come out perfectly cooked, buttery and full of flavor. Larger potatoes can be cut in half.

Enough for four people.

POTATO PIE

torta di patate

2lb potatoes, 4 tablespoons milk, 6 tablespoons butter, salt, pepper, nutmeg, 3 tablespoons bread crumbs, 3oz cheese (Gruyère or Bel Paese), 3oz cooked ham, smoked sausage or mortadella, 2 eggs.

Mash the boiled potatoes, add milk and 4 tablespoons butter; season with salt, pepper and nutmeg. Line an 8-inch pie plate with 1 tablespoon butter and half the bread crumbs. Spread a layer of potatoes smoothly into the tin. On top arrange the cheese and the ham cut into squares, and the 2 eggs, boiled for 6 minutes, shelled and cut into quarters. Cover the ham, cheese and eggs with the rest of the mashed potatoes. Spread the remaining bread crumbs on the top, pour over the remaining butter, melted, and cook the pie for about 40 minutes in a fairly hot oven (375°F).

Enough for five to six people.

SPINACH PIE

spanakopittá

This is a Greek (and also Turkish) dish made with filo pastry.

2lb spinach, 6 tablespoons butter, 12 sheets filo pastry leaves (thawed if frozen), ¼lb Gruyère cheese.

Clean and cook the spinach in the usual way, and squeeze it very dry. Chop it not too finely, and heat it in a pan with 2 tablespoons of butter. Season well. Butter a square cake pan, not too deep. In the bottom put 6 sheets of filo pastry cut to the shape of the pan and a fraction larger, brushing the top of each leaf with melted butter before covering it with the next sheet.

Over the 6 layers of pastry spread the prepared spinach, then a layer of the grated Gruyère. Cover with 6 more layers of pastry, again buttering between each layer, and buttering also the top. See that the edges of the pastry are also well buttered, and cook in a moderate oven, 350°F for 30–40 minutes. Leave to cool for a few minutes, turn upside down onto a baking sheet, slide back into the pan and return to the oven for 10 minutes or so for the underside to get crisp and golden.

Enough for four people.

SPINACH *with* GOLDEN RAISINS
spinaci con uvetta

2lb spinach, salt, 2 tablespoons butter, olive oil, a clove of garlic, pepper, 3 tablespoons golden raisins, 3 tablespoons pine nuts.

Clean the spinach and put it into a large saucepan with any clinging water and a little salt, but no additional water. Plenty of moisture comes out as it cooks. When it is cooked drain it, pressing it hard so that as much of the moisture as possible is removed. In a wide saucepan or frying pan warm the butter and 2 tablespoons of olive oil. Add the spinach, the chopped garlic and a little pepper. Turn the spinach over and over; it should not fry, and neither should the garlic. When it is thoroughly hot put in the raisins, which should have soaked for 15 minutes in a cup of warm water, and the pine nuts. Cover the pan, and continue to cook very gently for another 15 minutes.

Enough for two to three people.

MY DREAM KITCHEN

So frequently do dream kitchens figure in the popular newspaper competitions, in the pages of shiny magazines and in department store advertising that one almost begins to believe women really do spend half their days dreaming about laminated work-tops, louvered cupboard doors and sheaves of gladioli standing on top of the dishwasher. Why of all rooms in the house does the kitchen have to be a dream? Is it because in the past kitchens have mostly been so underprivileged, so dingy and inconvenient? We don't, for example, hear much of dream drawing-rooms, dream bedrooms, dream garages, dream storage rooms (I could do with a couple of those). No. It's a dream kitchen or nothing. My own kitchen is rather more of a nightmare than a dream, but I'm stuck with it. However, I'll stretch a point and make it a good dream for a change. Here goes.

This fantasy kitchen will be large, very light, very airy, calm and warm. There will be the minimum of paraphernalia in sight. It will start off and will remain rigorously orderly. That takes care of just a few desirable attributes my present kitchen doesn't have. Naturally there'll be, as now, a few of those implements in constant use—ladles, a sieve or two, whisks, tasting spoons—hanging by the stove, essential knives accessible in a rack, and wooden spoons in a jar. But half a dozen would be enough, not thirty-five as there are now. Cookery writers are particularly vulnerable to the acquisition of unnecessary clutter. I'd love to rid myself of it.

The sink will be a double one, with a solid wooden draining-board on each side. It will be (in fact, is) set 30 inches from the ground, about 6 inches higher than usual. I'm tall, and I didn't want to be prematurely bent double as a result of leaning over a knee-high sink. Along the wall above the sink I envisage a continuous wooden plate rack designed to hold serving dishes as well as plates, cups and other crockery in normal use. This saves a great deal of space, and much time spent getting out and putting away. Talking of space, suspended from the ceiling would be a wooden rack or slatted shelves—such as farmhouses and even quite small cottages in parts of Wales and the Midland counties used to have for storing bread or drying out oatcakes. Here would be the parking place for papers, notebooks, magazines—all the things that usually get piled on chairs when the table has to be cleared. The table itself is, of course, crucial. It's for writing at and for meals, as well as for kitchen tasks, so it has to have comfortable leg room. This time round I'd like it to be oval, one massive piece of scrubbable wood, on a central pedestal. Like the sink, it has to be a little higher than the average.

Outside the kitchen is my refrigerator and there it will stay. I keep it at the lowest temperature, about 40°F. I'm still amazed at the way so-called model kitchens have refrigerators next to the cooking stove. This seems to me almost as mad as having a wine rack above it. Then, failing a separate pantry—in a crammed London house that's carrying optimism a bit too far—there would be a second and fairly large refrigerator to be used for the cool storage of a variety of commodities such as coffee beans, spices, butter, cheese and eggs, which benefit from a constant temperature of 50°F.

All the colors in the dream kitchen would be much as they are now, but fresher and cleaner— cool silver, gray-blue, aluminium, with the various browns of earthenware pots and a lot of white provided by the perfectly plain china. I recoil from colored tiles and beflowered surfaces and I don't want a lot of things colored avocado and tangerine. I'll just settle for the avocados and tangerines in a bowl on the dresser. In other words, if the food and the cooking pots don't provide enough visual interest and create their own changing patterns in a kitchen, then there's something wrong. And too much equipment is if anything worse than too little. I don't a bit covet the exotic gear dangling from hooks, the riot of clanking ironmongery, the armories of knives, or the serried rank of sauté pans and all other carefully chosen symbols of culinary activity I see in so many photographs of chic kitchens. Pseuds corners, I'm afraid, many of them.

When it comes to the stove I don't think I need anything very fancy. My cooking is mostly on a small scale and of the kind for intimate friends, so I'm happy enough with an ordinary four-burner gas stove. Its oven has to be a good size, though, and it has to have a drop-down door. Given the space I'd have a second, quite separate oven just for bread, and perhaps some sort of temperature-controlled cupboard for proofing the dough. On the whole though it's probably best for cookery writers to use the same kind of domestic equipment as the majority of their readers. It doesn't do to get too far away from the problems of everyday household cooking or take the easy way out with expensive gadgetry.

What it all amounts to is that for me—and I stress this is purely personal, because my requirements as a writing cook are rather different from those of one who cooks mainly for a succession of guests or for the daily meals of a big family—the perfect kitchen would really be more like a painter's studio furnished with cooking equipment than anything conventionally accepted as a kitchen.

Article from Terence Conran's The Kitchen Book, *1977*

RICE

Every amateur cook, however gifted and diligent, has some weak spot, some gap in her knowledge or experience which to anyone critical of her own achievements can be annoying and humiliating. To some it may be a question of not being able to get a roast precisely right; to others, a cream sauce which only spasmodically comes off; and even to those who admit to having little talent for pastry or cakes, it is irritating to be defeated by a process which to others appears so effortless. Some regard the confection of a mayonnaise as the easiest thing in the world, some with terror and despair. There are those who have a talent for perfect rice dishes, while for others the stuff invariably turns to a mush. And it is no coincidence that when dishes go wrong, it nearly always happens when they are cooked for guests, and consequently in larger quantities than those with which one is accustomed to dealing.

Sometimes this is due to something so obvious as cooking for eight in the same utensils as those normally used for four, or to the cook having overlooked the fact that even a good-tempered dish like a meat and wine stew may disloyally change its character and appearance, losing all its professional-looking finish, if kept waiting too long in the oven. Or perhaps the roast, twice as large as usual, has been cooked twice as long, whereas what should really have been taken into consideration was not the weight but the shape and thickness of the roast.

Sometimes, of course, the trouble is more psychological than technical. Take rice, for example. Because a rice dish has gone wrong once, no doubt because the cook had no experience of cooking the particular rice she was using, she will ever after be scared stiff of making it. There is something rather specifically dismal about a failed rice dish. And I would never recommend anybody to cook a risotto for a dinner party which had to be managed single-handed, because it is a bad dish to keep waiting. But there are so many other ways of cooking rice and some of them appear to be specially designed for the kind of meals we all cook these days—meals consisting of dishes which simply must not be of the kind requiring split-second timing. Good-quality rice is essential, though. The two kinds to look for are the long-grained Patna type, of which basmati is the best, and the round-grained Piedmontese rice called avorio or arborio, which has a hard core in the center of the grain so that it is almost impossible to ruin by overcooking. The flavor of this Piedmontese rice is also much more pronounced than that of the Patna type, which makes it a good one to use when the rice itself, rather than any flavoring or sauce, is the main point of the dish.

A good point to remember about the boiling of rice is that ten times the volume of water to that of rice is an ample quantity to calculate. So measure the rice in a cup or glass, and then reckon the amount of water accordingly.

MILANESE RISOTTO
risotto alla milanese

Rice is to the northern provinces of Italy (Lombardy, Piedmont and the Veneto) what pasta is to the south. I wish I knew who was the genius who first grasped the fact that Piedmontese rice was ideally suited to slow cooking and that its particular qualities would be best appreciated in what has become the famous Milanese risotto. The fact that this rice can be cooked contrary to all rules, slowly, in a small amount of liquid, and emerge in a perfect state of creaminess with a very slightly resistant core in each grain gives the risotto its particular character.

The classic *risotto alla milanese* is made simply with chicken stock and flavored with saffron; butter and grated Parmesan cheese are stirred in at the end of the cooking, and more cheese and butter served with it. The second version is made with beef marrow and white wine; a third with Marsala. In each case saffron is used as a flavoring.

Into a heavy pan put 2 tablespoons *butter*. In the butter fry a *small onion* cut very fine; let it turn pale gold but not brown; then add 1oz of *beef marrow* extracted from marrow bones; this gives a richer quality to the risotto, but can perfectly well be left out. Now add *Italian rice*, allowing about 3oz (a heaping ⅓ cup) per person (in Italy they would allow a good deal more; the amount rather depends upon whether the risotto is to constitute a first course only or a main dish). Stir the rice until it is well impregnated with the butter. It must remain white.

Now pour in about ½ cup of *dry white wine* and let it cook on a moderate flame until the wine has almost evaporated. At this moment start adding the *stock*, which should be a light chicken consommé and which is kept barely simmering in another pan; add about a ladle at a time, and keep your eye on the risotto, although at this stage it is not essential to stir continuously. As the stock becomes absorbed add more; in all you will need about 5 cups of stock for 10–14oz (1½–2 cups) of rice, and if this is not quite enough, dilute it with hot water. Towards the end of the cooking, which will take 20–30 minutes, stir continuously using a wooden fork rather than a spoon, which tends to crush the grains. When you see that the rice is tender, the mixture creamy but not sticky, add the *saffron*.

The proper way to do this is to pound the strands to a powder (three or four strands will be enough for 2 cups of rice), steep the powder in about ½ cup of the stock for 5 minutes, and strain the liquid obtained into the rice. Having stirred in the saffron, add 2 tablespoons each of butter and grated *Parmesan cheese*, and serve the risotto as soon as the cheese has melted. More butter and grated cheese must be served separately.

Enough for four people.

RISOTTO *with* GREEN PEAS
risi e bisi

A small onion, 3 tablespoons butter, 2oz ham, 2lb green peas in the pod (or 2 cups shelled peas), 3¾ cups chicken or meat stock, 1½ cups of risotto rice, Parmesan cheese.

Put the chopped onion to melt in 1 tablespoon of butter. Add the chopped ham, which should be fat and lean in equal quantities. Let it melt slightly, add the shelled peas. When they are impregnated with the butter pour in 1½ cups of hot stock, and when it is bubbling, add the rice. Now pour over more hot stock, about 2¼ cups, and cook gently without stirring; before it is all absorbed, add more. *Risi e bisi* is not cooked in quite the same way as the ordinary risotto, for it should emerge rather more liquid; it should not be stirred too much or the peas will break. It is to be eaten, however, with a fork, not a spoon, so it must not be too soupy. When the rice is cooked stir in 2 tablespoons each of butter and grated Parmesan, and serve more cheese separately.

To make a less rich dish cook the rice with water instead of stock, which will produce soothing food for tired stomachs.

Enough for four to five people.

CHICKEN RISOTTO

risotto alla sbirraglia

Most recipes for chicken risotto require a chicken stock made from the bones of the bird, but in this case the liquid from the previously stewed pieces of chicken supplies sufficient richness, so that it is really preferable to use water and reserve the carcass and bones of the chicken for a soup.

Half a chicken, 2 small onions, butter or oil, a slice of prosciutto or mortadella, 3 or 4 tomatoes, a rib of celery, sliced, a clove of garlic, sliced, a green or red pepper, cleaned and cut into strips, a few dried porcini mushrooms, ⅔ cup dry white wine, seasoning and herbs, risotto rice, Parmesan cheese.

For four people use half a 3½lb chicken (the other half can be used for another meal).

Remove the skin, take all the flesh off the bones, and cut into fairly large, long slices. In a thick pan sauté a sliced onion in butter or oil, and when it is golden add the pieces of chicken, the chopped prosciutto, and the other vegetables. Let them fry for a few minutes, then pour in the wine, leaving it to bubble for 3 or 4 minutes. Add seasoning and fresh herbs (marjoram, thyme or basil). Add hot water barely to cover the contents of the pan, put on the lid, and cook very slowly for about 30 minutes, preferably in a low (300°F) oven. (This preparation can be made beforehand and heated when the time comes to make the risotto.)

For the risotto allow about 1½ cups of rice for four people. In a large, shallow and heavy pan heat 2 tablespoons of butter or olive oil, and in it melt the second onion, sliced very finely; add the rice and stir, allowing it to soak up the butter. Now add boiling water to cover the rice, stir again, and when the water is absorbed add more, cooking all the time over a moderate flame, and stirring frequently so that the rice does not stick. Season with a little salt. When you see that the rice is all but cooked pour in the chicken mixture, sauce and all, and continue stirring until the liquid is absorbed and the rice tender. At this moment stir in 2 tablespoons of grated Parmesan and 2 tablespoons of butter. The risotto can be served in the pan in which it has cooked, or it can be turned out onto a hot dish.

Enough for four people.

PILAF RICE

There are Egyptian, Turkish, Persian, Indian, Chinese and goodness knows how many other systems of cooking and flavoring pilaf rice. This is one of my own recipes, evolved by combining an Indian method with flavorings which are predominantly Levantine.

Measurements for pilaf rice cookery are nearly always based on volume rather than weight. The use of a cup or glass for measuring the rice simplifies the recipes because the cooking liquid is measured in the same vessel, the success of the process depending largely upon the correct proportions of liquid to rice. The cooking pot is also important, especially to those unfamiliar with the routine. Choose a saucepan or a two-handled casserole not too deep in proportion to its width. Whether of aluminium, iron, cast iron, copper or earthenware is not important provided the base is thick and even.

Those unfamiliar with rice cookery are advised to start by making a small quantity of pilaf, enough for say two or three people. The recipe once mastered, it is easy to increase the quantities, in proportion, and to experiment with different flavorings.

> *Using long-grain basmati rice the initial ingredients and preparations are as follows: 1 cup of rice, 2 cups of water.*
>
> For the flavoring: *2 tablespoons butter (or ghee bought from an Indian specialty store), 1 small onion, 4 cardamom pods, 2 teaspoons of cumin seeds, or ground cumin, 1 teaspoon of ground turmeric, 2 teaspoons of salt, 2 cups of water, a bay leaf or two.*

Put the rice in a bowl and cover it with water. Leave it to soak for an hour or so.

Melt the butter in your rice-cooking pot or saucepan (for this quantity a 6–8 cup one is large enough) and in it cook the sliced onion for a few minutes, until it is translucent. It must not brown. This done, stir in the cardamom seeds extracted from their pods and the cumin seeds, both pounded in a mortar, and the turmeric. The latter is for coloring the rice a beautiful yellow, as well as for its flavor, and the object of cooking the spices in the fat is to develop their aromas before the rice is added. This is an important point.

Drain the rice, and put it into the butter and spice mixture. Stir it around until it glistens with the fat. Add the salt. Pour in the water and let it come to the boil fairly fast. Put in the bay leaf.

Let the rice cook steadily, uncovered, over a medium heat until almost all the water is absorbed and holes begin to appear in the mass. This will take almost 10 minutes.

Now turn the heat as low as possible. Over the rice put a thickly folded absorbent kitchen towel, and on top of the cloth (use an old one; the turmeric stains) the lid of the pan. Leave undisturbed, still over the lowest possible heat, for 20–25 minutes. At the end of this time the rice should be quite tender and each grain will be separated. Fork it round, turn into a warmed serving bowl. The rice should be a fine yellow color and mildly spiced.

The pilaf can be eaten as an accompaniment to spiced lamb or beef kebabs, but to my mind is even nicer on its own, with the addition of a few golden or seedless raisins, soaked for an hour in water, heated up in a little saucepan and mixed into the rice just before it is turned out of the saucepan for serving. Oven-toasted almonds or pine nuts make another attractive addition.

Enough for four people.

QUICK KEDGEREE

For a party I make a kedgeree [a Raj dish that is a very popular buffet item for British brunch and supper] with rice boiled in advance, then kept hot, with all its extra ingredients, in a big bowl standing in a saucepan of simmering water.

For an impromptu dish for two or three people I use a quick and easy method which, once you've understood the principle, has infinite possibilities. You can apply the same system to shrimp, mussels, vegetables, chicken, meat—with one proviso. Good-quality rice, either long-grained basmati or the hard round-grained Italian variety is essential. Soft pudding rice will turn to just that—pudding.

> *3 smoked haddock fillets, 2 tablespoons olive oil, 1 medium onion, a scant teaspoon curry powder, ½ cup rice, 2 tablespoons golden raisins or currants, water, seasonings, 2 hard-boiled eggs, parsley, a lemon, butter (optional), mango chutney.*

First pour boiling water over the haddock fillets. Leave them 2 or 3 minutes, drain them, peel off the skin and divide the fish into manageable pieces.

Heat the oil in a heavy 10-inch frying or sauté pan. In this fry the sliced onion until pale yellow. Stir in the curry powder. Add the rice (don't wash it). Stir all round together. Add the washed raisins or currants. Pour in 2¼ cups of water. Cook steadily, not at a gallop, and uncovered, for 10 minutes. Put in the haddock. Continue cooking until the liquid is all absorbed and the rice tender—approximately 10 minutes. But keep an eye on it to see it doesn't stick, and stir with a fork, not a spoon, which breaks the rice. Taste for seasoning. Salt may or may not be required. Turn onto a hot serving dish. On the top strew the quartered eggs and parsley—and, if you like, a nice big lump of butter. Surround with lemon quarters and serve with mango chutney.

Enough for four people.

SPICED RICE *with* LENTILS
khichri

The dish from which the English evolved kedgeree. The original contains no fish, and is simply a mixture of lentils and rice cooked with spices. It is very cheap and filling.

Khichri can be eaten on its own or as an accompaniment to a meat or chicken curry. In either case a little dish of chutney and another of fresh cucumber with a yogurt and mint dressing or some other such refreshing little preparation should be offered at the same time. The spices can be altered to suit individual taste. Those who do not like ginger or cloves could substitute cumin and turmeric, and if you have no cardamom seeds—well, perhaps you will invent some new and perfect spice mixture. If English kedgeree can evolve from *khichri*, then in cookery anything at all can happen.

> *6 allspice berries, 6 white peppercorns, the seeds from 6 cardamom pods, ¼ teaspoon each of ground ginger and cloves, ⅔ cup clarified butter or ghee, 1 small onion, 2 tablespoons each of red lentils and basmati rice, salt, a tablespoon or two of the liquid part of rather sharp mango chutney or, more correctly, of tamarind pulp, 2⅔ cups of water, lemon juice.*

Pound the allspice, peppercorns and cardamoms. Mix them with the ground spices.

In the clarified butter or ghee melt the thinly sliced onion. Do not let it brown. Stir in the spices, let them fry for a minute or so. Add the lentils, then the rice. Stir both round in the fat. Season with salt—about 1½ teaspoons. Add the chutney or tamarind pulp. Pour in the cold water.

Cook, uncovered, over medium heat. Stir from time to time with a fork, for about 15 minutes, until all the water is absorbed. By this time the lentils are nearly cooked but the rice is not. Turn the heat as low as possible, put the saucepan on a heat-diffuser mat, cover the rice and lentils with a folded kitchen towel and the lid of the saucepan. Leave for 20 minutes. Turn into a heated dish, squeeze lemon juice over and serve at once, very hot.

There should be enough for three or four, depending upon what other dishes are to be given.

ITALIAN FISH MARKETS

Of all the spectacular food markets in Italy, the one near the Rialto in Venice must be the most remarkable. The light of a Venetian dawn in early summer—you must be about at four o'clock in the morning to see the market coming to life—is so limpid and so still that it makes every separate vegetable and fruit and fish luminous with a life of its own, with unnaturally heightened colors and clear stencilled outlines. Here the cabbages are cobalt blue, the beets deep rose, the lettuces clear pure green, sharp as glass. Bunches of gaudy gold zucchini flowers show off the elegance of pink and white marbled bean pods, primrose potatoes, green plums, green peas. The colors of the peaches, cherries and apricots, packed in boxes lined with sugar-bag blue paper matching the blue canvas trousers worn by the men unloading the gondolas, are reflected in the rose-red mullet and the orange *vongole* and *canuestrelle* which have been prised out of their shells and heaped into baskets. In other markets, on other shores, the unfamiliar fishes may be vivid, mysterious, repellent, fascinating, and bright with splendid color; only in Venice do they look good enough to eat. In Venice even ordinary sole and ugly great skate are striped with delicate lilac lights, the sardines shine like newly minted silver coins, pink Venetian scampi are fat and fresh, infinitely enticing in the early dawn.

The gentle swaying of the laden gondolas, the movements of the market men as they unload, swinging the boxes and baskets ashore, the robust life and rattling noise contrasted with the fragile taffeta colors and the opal sky of Venice—the whole scene is out of some marvelous unheard-of ballet.

A very different kettle of fish, indeed, is the market of Genoa. Nothing will shake my conviction that *Genova la superba* is the noisiest city on earth. (This is nothing new; travellers have constantly remarked upon the fact.) The market place will therefore be quite a rest; here one is oblivious of the uproar, spellbound by the spectacle of the odd fish which come up from these waters. Their names are descriptive enough: the angler or frogfish, the praying-fish, the sea hen, the scorpion, the sea cat, the sea date, the sea truffle, sea snails, sea strawberries, and a mussel with a hair-covered shell called *cozze pelose*. No wonder that anybody with a spark of imagination is prepared to put up with the ear-splitting din of Genoa, the crashing of trams and trains, the screeching of brakes, and even the agonized wailing of itinerant musicians in the taverns, in order to taste some of these sea beasts when they have been converted into *burrida*, the Genoese fish stew, or into the immense edifice of crustaceans, mollusks, fish, vegetables and green sauce, which is known as *cappon magro*.

Along the coast at Santa Margherita the fish market is famous; here the fish are less forbidding and savage of aspect, but their brilliance of color is phenomenal. Huge baskets are filled with what from a distance one takes to be strawberries but which turn out to be huge shrimp (they are scarlet by nature, before they are cooked); dark green and grey *tonnetto*, gleaming silver with phosphorescence, are thrust head downwards, like so many French loaves, in a high basket; *moscardini*, brown and pale green, are arranged in rows, like newly washed pebbles; the tiny *calamaretti*, *fragoline di mare*, are black and grey (cooked in a wine sauce they turn a deep pink); the rose-colored slippery little fish called *signorini* are for the *frittura*; the scampi are pallid compared to the brilliant shrimp; an orange *langouste* is a tamed beast beside a black lobster, lashing furiously.

Another market with its own very characteristic flavor is that of Cagliari, in the island of Sardinia. Spread out in flat baskets large as cartwheels are all the varieties of fish which go into *ziminù*, the Sardinian version of fish soup; fat, scaly little silver fish streaked with lime green; enormous octopus, blue, sepia, mauve and turquoise, curled and coiled and petalled like some heavily embroidered marine flower; the *pescatrice* again, that ugly hooked angler fish; cold stony little clams, here called *arselle*; *tartufi di mare*; silvery slippery sardines; rose-red mullets in every possible size, some small as sprats, like doll's-house fish; the fine lobsters for which Sardinia is famous. To eat the plainly grilled or fried fish in this island is an experience from which any town dweller, accustomed to fish which must have been in the ice at least a day or two, will derive great pleasure. The mullet, the thin slices of fresh tuna, the little clams, seem to have been washed straight from the sea into the frying pan, so fresh and tender is their flesh. In such conditions there is no necessity to create complicated sauces and garnishes; and, indeed, for the cooking of fish Italian cooks are mainly content to concentrate their skill on the arts of frying, grilling and roasting.

from Italian Food, *1954*

FISH,
SHELLFISH
and
CRUSTACEA

Boiled salmon with cucumber and mayonnaise is an admirable dish, but anyone visiting Britain for the first time and dining out frequently might well be excused for supposing that salmon is the only fish procurable in England during the whole of the summer. In fact, salmon is at its best in the very early spring; later, it scarcely justifies its high price. Salmon trout, in season all summer until the end of August, is an exquisite fish. If it is a cold dish that is needed and there is money to spend, fillets of sole make a very welcome change from the eternal salmon. Then there are some excellent lesser-known fish, such as John Dory, sea bream (porgy), Cornish bass and grey mullet which are comparatively cheap; so it is well worth knowing how to deal with them.

Rock salmon and mackerel make good cheap cold dishes, and red mullet, although more expensive, makes one of the best and most beautiful of summer fish dishes when grilled on a bed of dried fennel stalks. Fresh brown trout fried or grilled and served with plenty of melted butter are a rare treat, but the little rainbow trout are often rather disappointing. An interesting sauce, however, does a great deal for them. A grilled herring has always seemed to me one of those cheap luxuries of which there are all too few; herrings are out of season in May and June, but later in the summer they can be enjoyed with fresh herbs and butter and perhaps French mustard. Remember soft herring roes too; with a little ingenuity they make most excellent little dishes, at a very small cost.

Crabs are useful for all sorts of soups, salads and soufflés, but a little, unlike other crustaceans of which one needs a lot, goes a long way. Unless you know your fishmonger pretty well, it is not advisable to buy "dressed" crab from him; it is often mixed with bread, and sometimes not of the first freshness.

For those who like fish plain grilled, fried, baked or poached, there are the delicious classic French sauces, hollandaise, maltaise, Bercy, remoulade, and a few lesser-known sauces made with herbs, almonds, walnuts, avocados, which will often liven up a rather dull fish. Of all vegetables, I think perhaps sorrel is the one which goes best with coarse fish. Spinach not being a good substitute, the next best vegetables are tomatoes, and, for more delicate fish, mushrooms, lettuce, zucchini, and watercress cooked a few seconds in butter, then chopped.

GRILLED RED MULLET *with* AÏOLI *and* SAUCE ROUILLE

rougets à la provençale

For the aïoli: *2 large cloves of garlic pounded in a mortar, 2 egg yolks, a little salt, a generous ¾ cup of olive oil, mixed exactly as for a Mayonnaise (see page 299).*

For the red part of the sauce: *2 medium (8oz) grilled and skinned red peppers pounded with a teaspoon of paprika, add ¾ cup of fresh bread crumbs, softened in water, then pressed dry, to the pounded peppers.*

Score large *red mullets* (or other smallish fish) obliquely, twice, on each side, and paint them with *olive oil*. Grill them for about 10 minutes on each side and serve with a combination of two Provençal sauces, *aïoli* and *sauce rouille*. At the last minute amalgamate the two sauces, adding the *aïoli* gradually to the pepper mixture. Gray mullet may be served in the same way.

Allow one fish, or half if very large, per person.

BAKED PORGY

Marinate a medium to large *porgy* for an hour in *olive oil* and *lemon juice*, with a *bay leaf*, *parsley*, *thyme*, *salt* and *pepper*.

Cook it in an open baking dish in a fairly hot oven, at 375°F, so that the skin gets nicely golden and crackling.

Serve with the following sauce: a chopped *shallot* in a glass of *white wine* reduced to half: add ½ teaspoon of *Dijon mustard*, 4 tablespoons of *butter*, 2 pounded *hard-boiled egg yolks*, *salt*, *pepper* and *chopped parsley*.

A large gray mullet may be cooked in the same way, but make sure it is very well cleaned, and washed under running water, as these fish sometimes have a slightly muddy taste.
Enough for two to three people.

GRAY MULLET *with* OLIVES *and* WHITE WINE
mulet aux olives et au vin blanc

A very simple and effective recipe which can be applied to many sorts of fish, including red mullet, porgy, sea bass, whiting and mackerel.

> *2 medium-sized fish, each weighing approximately 1lb before cleaning, 5 tablespoons olive oil, a little sprig of thyme or fennel or a bay leaf, salt and pepper, 2 to 5 tablespoons dry white wine, a dozen pitted black olives, some slices of orange or lemon.*

Put the cleaned fish into a shallow oval ovenproof dish, pour the oil over them, add your herbs, a sprinkling of salt and pepper and the white wine. Bake, uncovered, for 15–20 minutes in a medium oven at 375°F.

Now add the pitted black olives and cook another 5 minutes. The mullet can be served in the dish in which they have cooked, or be transferred to a flat serving dish, in either case with their own juice and slices of orange or lemon arranged along each fish. May be served hot or cold.

Enough for two to three people.

SEA BASS *with* MUSHROOMS *and* POTATOES

bar à la marseillaise

Bar or *loup de mer* is one of the most delicate fish of the Mediterranean; grilled on a bed of fennel stalks it makes the famous Provençal *grillade au fenouil*.

A bass weighing 2½–3lb, cleaned, ½ cup olive oil, ¼ cup dry white wine, a little bouquet of fennel leaves, 2 cloves of garlic, ½lb onions, ½lb mushrooms, 1lb yellow waxy potatoes, salt and pepper.

Put the fish in a baking dish, pour over it the oil and wine, cover with the chopped fennel and garlic, round it arrange the sliced onions, mushrooms and thinly sliced potatoes. Season with salt and pepper, add 2¼ cups of water and cook in a fairly hot oven, at 375°F for about an hour.

Serve with an *aïoli* or *rouille* (see recipe for Grilled Red Mullet with Aïoli and Sauce Rouille, page 178).

Enough for four people.

BAKED SALMON TROUT

truite saumonée au four

Few of us now possess fish kettles in which a large whole fish can be poached, but the system of wrapping the fish in parchment paper or foil and cooking it in the oven produces, if anything, better results. Sea bass (*loup de mer*) is excellent cooked in the same way.

Cut a piece of parchment paper or aluminium foil about 6 inches longer than your *salmon trout*. *Butter* it copiously, or if the fish is to be served cold, paint it with *oil*. Lay the fish in the middle, gather up the edges and twist them together, so that no juices can escape. Also twist the two ends very securely, taking particular care that the paper touching the tail and the head is well buttered or oiled, as these are the parts which stick easily.

Have your oven already heated for 10 minutes at a very low temperature, 275°F. Place your wrapped fish on a baking sheet and leave it severely alone for the whole cooking time— 1 hour for a 2-lb fish. All you have to do when it is cooked is to lay it on a warmed serving dish, unwrap the paper and slide the fish and all its juices off the paper onto the dish. A hot salmon trout does not really need any sauce other than its own juices and a little bowl of fresh melted butter. If it is to be served cold, have with it a Green Sauce (page 300) or, best of all, I think, Walnut and Horseradish Sauce (page 304). It also makes serving easier if the skin is removed while the fish is still warm; this is not difficult so long as the fish has not been overcooked but, of course, it must be done gently and patiently.

There is one more point. A cold salmon trout eaten a couple of hours after it is cooked is infinitely superior to one cooked and kept until the following day.

FILLETS *of* SOLE *with* CREAM *and* ONION SAUCE

filets de sole deauvillaise

Sole cooked *à la deauvillaise* is a curious combination, perhaps, but one much liked by those who share the Norman fondness for onions.

Fillets of John Dory, sea bream, whiting or even plaice can be prepared in this way.

> *1 medium onion, butter, 2 fine soles, filleted, ⅔ cup hard cider or white wine, lemon, salt, 1¼ cups heavy cream, nutmeg, pepper, Dijon mustard, fresh bread crumbs.*

Chop the onion after it has been peeled. Melt 3 tablespoons of butter in a thick pan; in this cook the onions very gently, so that they turn transparent and yellow but not brown. In the meantime make a little fish stock by cooking the carcasses of the soles for 10 minutes with ⅔ cup cider or white wine, 1¼ cups of water, a slice of lemon and a little salt. Strain. Purée the onions, add about 2 tablespoons of the prepared stock and the cream; stir till smooth and fairly thick. Season with grated nutmeg, a little freshly ground pepper, salt if necessary and a scant teaspoon of Dijon mustard. All this can be done in advance.

When the time comes to cook the fish, poach the fillets in the remainder of the stock. About 5 minutes is enough. Remove them to a heated oval gratin dish. Cover them with the sauce, gently reheated. Sprinkle bread crumbs on the top, and add a few little pieces of butter. Put under the broiler for about 3 minutes and serve at once, with little triangles of bread fried in butter arranged round the dish.

Enough for four people.

TURBOT *with* CREAM *and* HERB SAUCE

turbot sauce messine

For those who can lay hands on tarragon and chervil, a herb and cream mixture called *sauce messine*, from Lorraine, is one of the most delicious of summer sauces to serve with fish. Buy a piece of turbot weighing a little over 2lb (the bones are very large, so this is not too much for four people).

First chop together the leaves of half a dozen sprigs of *tarragon*, the same of *parsley* and *chervil* and 2 small *shallots*. Then work together 4 tablespoons of *butter* and a teaspoon of *flour*, add a teaspoon of *Dijon mustard*, two beaten *egg yolks* and 1¼ cups of *half and half*. Blend with the herb and shallot mixture, season, and put all in a small saucepan. Heat with the saucepan standing in hot water, stirring all the time until the sauce thickens. Do not let it boil. Put the *turbot* in a baking dish and cover it completely with half water and half *milk*. Cut turbot is much apt to dry up during cooking, and so should have plenty of moisture. Add *salt* and a sprig of fresh tarragon and parsley.

Bake, covered with buttered parchment or waxed paper, in a fairly slow oven, 325°F, for about 55 minutes, until you see that the flesh comes easily away from the bones. One side of the turbot is thicker than the other, so the timing depends a little bit on whether you have a thick or thin piece. Lift out the fish onto a hot serving dish, and have the sauce ready to be served separately. Immediately before serving, squeeze in the juice of a small *lemon*.

FISHERMAN'S CLAMS
vongole alla marinara

A rough and ready dish, often served in seaport taverns. Even in London mussels cooked in this way preserve a good deal of their flavor of the sea.

Wash and scrub 2½ quarts (at least 1½ dozen per person) of *little clams* (or mussels) and put them to open in a heavy pan over a fairly hot flame. They are to cook in their own liquid only. Cover the pan to start with, and take the lid off when the shells start to open. At this moment add *chopped parsley* and *garlic*.

Serve as soon as all the clams are opened, with their own juice.

Enough for three to four people.

SCALLOPS *with* WHITE WINE *and* PANCETTA

Here is an excellent little scallop dish; the mixture of pancetta with the fish sounds odd, but it is an old-fashioned and good one.

1 tablespoon butter, a shallot or two, 2oz pancetta, 4 large scallops, pepper,
1 teaspoon all-purpose flour, ⅓ cup dry white wine, parsley.

Melt the butter in a frying pan, put in the finely chopped shallots and the pancetta cut into tiny cubes. Cut the cleaned scallops into larger cubes, season them with pepper but no salt, sprinkle them with flour and put them in the pan when the shallots have turned pale yellow and the pork is beginning to frizzle. Cook very gently for 2–3 minutes, then lift the scallops out with a slotted spoon and put them in a serving dish. Add the wine to the pan, boil to reduce a little while stirring; pour the sauce over the scallops and serve, garnished with parsley.

Enough for two people.

MUSSELS *with* SPICED RICE
moules au riz à la basquaise

In small quantities this dish is excellent hot or cold, as a starter. In larger quantities it makes a nice party dish. The quantity of liquid is always twice that of the volume of rice – i.e. 4 cups of stock, including the olive oil, to 2 cups of rice.

> *1½ cups long-grain basmati rice, 2¾ cups veal or fish stock and ¼ cup olive oil, 3–4oz chorizo sausage (or other coarse pork sausage), half a red or green pepper, paprika, about 3 dozen mussels, 8 shrimp, lemon.*

Boil the rice for 7 minutes in plenty of water, without salt. Drain it, and hold the colander under the running cold tap until all starch is washed away.

Put it in an earthenware or other ovenproof dish with the stock, the olive oil, the sausage cut into little cubes, the pepper, freed of all seeds and core, sliced into thin rounds, and a teaspoon of paprika. Bring to simmering point on top of the stove. Cover with a folded cloth, a lid, and put in a moderate oven, at 350°F. In 20–25 minutes the rice will have absorbed all the liquid and be beautifully cooked and well spiced. Open the mussels in a pan over a hot flame, with just a little water, and leave them in their shells. Gently fry the shrimp in a little oil. Turn the rice into a hot shallow dish, add the mussels and the shrimp. Garnish with quarters of lemon.

Enough for four people.

MOULES MARINIÈRE

There are several versions of *moules marinière*. Here are three of them.

1 small onion, 1 clove of garlic, a small rib of celery, ⅓ cup dry white wine, pepper, about 6 dozen mussels, 2 tablespoons butter, 1½ tablespoons all-purpose flour, parsley.

Put the chopped onion, garlic and celery into a large pan with the white wine and about 2¼ cups of water. Add pepper but not salt. Put in the well-cleaned mussels, cover the pan and cook until the shells open. Take out the mussels, keep them hot, and thicken the liquid in which they have cooked with 2 tablespoons soft butter and 1 tablespoon of flour, mashed into a paste and whisked into the pan. Pour the sauce over the mussels in a large tureen and sprinkle with parsley. Serve very hot.

To be eaten out of soup plates, with a fork and a soup spoon.

Another way is to prepare the sauce first; make a little white roux in the pan with butter, flour, chopped onion and celery and the white wine. Add 2¼ cups of water and cook until the liquid has the consistency of a thin soup. Put in the mussels. The mussels can then be served directly as they are opened, a great advantage, as they then do not lose their freshness and savor, which they are apt to do if they are reheated. On no account must the sauce be over-thickened, or you will simply have mussels in a white sauce.

Perhaps the most usual way of cooking *moules marinière* is simply to put the mussels into the pan with the white wine but no water, throw chopped parsley and onion or garlic over them as they are opening and serve as soon as they are all open.

Always serve plenty of French bread with *moules marinière*.

Enough for four to six people.

RAGOÛT *of* SHELLFISH

12 cooked extra-large shrimp or langoustines, 4 dozen mussels, 1 onion,
2 tablespoons butter, 1 tablespoon tomato paste, 4 cloves of garlic, seasoning,
2 teaspoons sugar, tarragon, 1 tablespoon all-purpose flour, 1¼ cups dry
white wine, ¼lb mushrooms, 6 scallops, lemon juice, parsley.

First of all split the shrimp in half, retaining 6 halves in their shells for the garnish. From the remaining shells remove the flesh and cut it into fairly large pieces. Clean the mussels carefully.

In a deep pan sauté a sliced onion in butter. When golden add the tomato paste, the chopped garlic, salt, pepper and the sugar and tarragon. Cook for 5 minutes. Stir in the flour. When thick, pour over the heated wine, and cook this sauce for 15–20 minutes. Add the flesh of the shrimp, the sliced mushrooms, the scallops cut into 2 rounds each, and the mussels. Turn up the heat and cook until the mussels have opened. At the last minute add the reserved shrimp in their shells. Turn into a deep dish, squeeze over a little lemon, sprinkle with chopped parsley and serve very hot, in soup plates.

The black shells of the mussels and the pink of the shrimp make a very decorative dish. The tails of large crawfish (or small lobster tails) can be used instead of the shrimp, but of course fewer will be needed, and they can be cut into four or six pieces each.

Enough for four to six people as a first course.

LOBSTER *with* TARRAGON–MUSTARD SAUCE

homard à la courchamps

This is not a classic regional or other recognized traditional dish, so you can call it what you please. It has no name of its own. I have named it after the Comte de Courchamps, author of the first of the three books in which I found the recipe. The others were by Dumas the Elder and the Baron Brisse. Highly imaginative as they were, all three gentlemen called it Sauce for Boiled Lobster.

> *1 freshly boiled, medium large (1½lb) lobster, 2 small shallots, 1 heaped teaspoon tarragon leaves, 2 tablespoons chopped parsley, salt, pepper, a scant teaspoon of strong yellow Dijon mustard, 24–30 drops of soy sauce, approximately 6 tablespoons mildly fruity Provence olive oil, the juice of half a rather small lemon, 1 teaspoon anisette de Bordeaux.*

From the split lobster extract all the red and creamy parts. Pound them in a mortar. Mix with the finely chopped shallots, tarragon and parsley. Add the seasonings and the soy sauce, then gradually stir in the olive oil; add lemon juice. Finally, the anisette. Divide the sauce into two portions, and serve it in little bowls or squat glasses placed on each person's plate, so that the lobster can be dipped into it. The lobster meat can be cut into scallops and piled neatly back into the shells.

Apart from its sheer deliciousness (most cold lobster sauces, including mayonnaise, are on the heavy side for what is already rich and solid food) this sauce has other points to recommend it. Anisette is not a liqueur which, speaking at least for myself, one has a great compulsion to swig down in quantity; in my cupboard a bottle lasts for years. A small bottle of soy sauce keeps almost indefinitely, and fresh tarragon can now be bought all year. The makings of your sauce, then, are always with you. All you need is the freshly boiled lobster.

Enough for two people.

SPINY LOBSTER *in* TOMATO *and* BRANDY SAUCE

langouste comme chez nénette

This dish comes from the port of Sète in the Languedoc and is a variation of the better-known *homard à l'américaine*. I have quoted the recipe given to me by Madame Nénette from her restaurant. [In France, Madame Nénette used a spiny lobster (*langouste*), but in the U.S., an Atlantic lobster works well, too.]

"Cut a live *lobster* into not too large pieces; put them at once into a wide and shallow pan containing a little smoking *olive oil*, add *salt* and *pepper* and cook until the shell turns red. Add some finely chopped *shallots* and a clove or two of *garlic*, crushed and first cooked separately in a little oil.

"Pour in a small glass of good *Cognac* and set light to it; when the flames have gone out, add a half bottle of still *Champagne or Chablis*, and a spoonful of *tomato paste*. Cover the pan and cook over a steady fire for about 20 minutes. Remove the pieces of lobster, which are now cooked, and keep them hot.

"Press the sauce through a very fine sieve, let it boil up again, season with a scrap of *cayenne* and, at the last minute, add 3 good spoonfuls of Aïoli. [See page 303.]

"Pour the sauce over the lobster and sprinkle a little finely chopped *parsley* over the dish."

Enough for two people.

SLOW-COOKED SQUID
calamari in umido

*1lb squid, salt, lemon juice, 2 large onions, oil, 2 or 3 tomatoes, marjoram
and thyme, 3 cloves of garlic, ½ cup red wine, 2 teaspoons tomato paste.*

To clean the squid, remove the insides from the pocket-like part of the fish, and pull out the
thin transparent spine bone. Remove also the purplish outside skin, which comes off very
easily in warm water.

From each side of the head remove the little ink bag (the whole operation is carried out in
a bowl of water and is very quickly done) and take out the eyes and the hard beak-like object
in the centre of the tentacles of which Dumas remarks that it is "*non pas un nez, mais l'anus (au
milieu du visage!)*." Rinse the squid in running water until it is quite free of grit. When clean
they are milky white.

Cut the body of the squid into rings, about ¼ inch wide, and the tentacles into strips.
Season them with salt and lemon juice. Now put the onions, cut into rings, into a pan in
which you have warmed enough olive oil to cover the bottom. Let them turn golden and add
the squid. After 2 minutes put in the chopped tomatoes, some marjoram and thyme, and
the garlic, and after 2 more minutes pour in the red wine; let this reduce a little and add the
2 teaspoons, not more, of the tomato paste. Add enough hot water to reach the level of the
ingredients in the pan, put on the lid, and cook very slowly for 1½ hours. Serve with rice or
with toasted French bread.

Enough for two to three people.

DISHES *for* COLLECTORS

A dish of pork and prunes seems a strange one to chase two hundred miles across France, and indeed it was its very oddity that sent me in search of it. The combination of meat with fruit is not only an uncommon one in France, it is one which the French are fond of citing as an example of the barbaric eating habits of other nations, the Germans and the Americans in particular. So to find such a dish in Tours, the very heart of sane and sober French cookery, is surprising, even given the fact that the local prunes are so renowned.

I knew where we would go to look for the dish because I had seen it on the menu of the Rôtisserie Tourangelle on a previous occasion, when there were so many other interesting specialities that it just hadn't been possible to get round to the *quasi de porc aux pruneaux*. But this time I hoped perhaps to find out how the dish was cooked as well as in what manner such a combination had become acceptable to conservative French palates.

Driving out of Orléans towards Tours I observed for the first time the ominous entry in the new *Guide Michelin* concerning the Rôtisserie Tourangelle: "*Déménagement prévu,*" it said. Very well, we would get to Tours early, we would enquire upon entering the town whether by some ill-chance the restaurant was at this moment in the throes of house-moving. If so, we would not stay in Tours, but console ourselves by driving on to Langeais, where there was a hotel whose cooking was said to be worth the journey. The evening was to be our last before driving north towards Boulogne, so we specially didn't want to make a hash of it. But we had plenty of time, the afternoon was fine, the Loire countryside lay before us in all its shining early summer beauty. We dawdled along, making a detour to Chenonceaux on the way.

So in the end it was after seven o'clock by the time we had battled into the main street of Tours, found the Office of the Syndicat d'Initiative, and made our enquiry. No, said the pretty and efficient young lady in charge, the house-moving of the Rôtisserie Tourangelle had not yet started. All was well. "*Déménagement prévu*, indeed," said my companion, "what a fuss. It'll be *prévu* for the next two years." Fifteen minutes later the car had been maneuvered into the courtyard of the charming Hotel Central, we had booked our room, the luggage was unloaded. As we were about to get into the lift I returned to the desk and asked the lady in charge if she would be so kind as to telephone chez Charvillat and book us a table, for we were already late. As I walked away, I heard her saying into the telephone "*Comment, vous êtes fermé?*"

Yes, the *déménagement* had started that day. Closed for a fortnight. Well it was hardly the fault of the charming girl at the Syndicat, but . . . anyway, it was now too late to move on to Langeais. We must eat at Tours and make the best of it. By the time I had explained the magnitude of the disaster to Madame at the desk, she and I were both nearly in tears. For she perfectly grasped the situation, and did not think it at all odd that we had driven two hundred miles simply to eat chez Charvillat. But all the restaurants in Tours, she said, were good. We would eat well wherever we went. Yes, but would we find that dish of *porc aux pruneaux* which by this time had become an obsession? And in any case what restaurant could possible be as nice, charming, as comfortable, as altogether desirable as that of M. Charvillat?

Madame spent the next twenty minutes telephoning round Tours on our behalf, and eventually sent us, somewhat consoled, to a well-known restaurant only two minutes' walk from the hotel. I wish I could end this story by saying that the place was a find, a dazzling revelation, a dozen times better than the one we had missed. But it was not as dramatic as that. It was indeed a very nice restaurant, the head waiter was friendly, and we settled down to some entirely entrancing white Vouvray while they cooked our *alose á l'oseille*—shad grilled and served with a sauce in the form of a runny sorrel purée. In this respect at least we had timed things properly, for the shad makes only a short seasonal appearance in the Loire. It was extremely good and nothing like as bony as shad is advertised to be. Then came this restaurant's version of the famous pork dish, which turned out to be made with little noisettes of meat in a very remarkable sauce and of course we immediately felt reproved for doubting for one moment that an intelligent French cook could make something splendid out of even such lumpish sounding ingredients as pork and prunes.

It was worth all the fuss, even for the sauce alone. But, almost inevitably, it was something of an anticlimax. The combination of a long day's drive, the sampling during the day of the lovely, poetical wines of Pouilly and of Sancerre *sur place* (and whatever anyone may say, they do taste different on the spot), a hideously ill-advised cream cake at an Orléans patisserie, the alternating emotions of triumph and despair following so rapidly one upon the other, not to mention a very large helping of the shad and sorrel, had wrecked our appetites. By this time it was known throughout the restaurant that some English had arrived especially to eat the *porc aux pruneaux*. The helpings, consequently, were very large. By the time we had eaten through it and learned how it was cooked, we were near collapse, but the *maître-d'hôtel* and the *patronne* were just warming up. If we were interested in local recipes, what about their *brochet au beurre blanc* and their *poulet á l'estragon*, and their *dodine de canard*? To be sure, we should have had that duck as an hors d'œuvre, but just a slice or two now, to taste, and then at least we would have some local cheeses and a sweet?

Curiosity overcame prudence. We did indeed try their *dodine de canard,* which was not the daube of duck in red wine usually associated with this name, but a very rich cold duck galantine, which would have been delicious as an hors d'œuvre, but after all that pork . . . Cravenly, we ordered coffee. No salad? No cheese? No dessert?

As we paid our bill, expressed our thanks, and left with the best grace we could muster, I was miserably aware that we had failed these kindly hospitable people and left them with the feeling that we did not appreciate their food.

It was a long time before I had the courage to set to work on that recipe. When I did, and saw once more the row of little pork noisettes, the bronze and copper lights of the shining sauce, the orderly row of black, rich, wine-soaked prunes on the long white dish, I thought that indeed it had been worth the journey to learn how to make something as beautiful as that. One day, with a better appetite and more stamina, I will go back to that restaurant in Tours and make amends for the evening when justice to their cookery was not done.

(See pages 250–51 for the pork and prunes recipe.)

from Vogue. *November 1958*

MEAT

French cooks, it is sometimes alleged, have perfected their particular brand of magic with second-class materials because they have no first-class ones. This, of course, is nonsensical. French cooks hold good-quality materials in the highest esteem, and certainly have plenty to work with. But the attitude of a French cook or housewife is extremely realistic. Appreciating the fact that not every fish that comes out of the sea is a sole, and that not even carefully nurtured animals are entirely constructed of prime steaks and cutlets, they have made it their business to know how to present coarser fish, elderly birds and second- or third-grade cuts of meat with the identical skill and ceremony accorded to luxury roasts and showpieces.

A good French butcher takes as much trouble over the cutting, trimming and presentation of his cheap cuts as with the prime roasts. Such things as shoulder and breast of lamb, shoulder cuts, skirt and briskets of beef, shins of veal and belly of pork are so neatly prepared that when the housewife buys them she knows exactly what she is getting; there will be no trimming or boning for her to do at home and so no waste, of either time or materials. Beef for braising or for *bœuf mode*, *bœuf bourguignon* or the *pot-au-feu* will be on display at the butcher's without her having to order it specially, to have it larded or to explain what is to be done. And this is where we come up against a difficulty when we want to cook French meat dishes in England, for it is not only the meticulous cutting and seaming, trimming and larding and tying which is differently approached in France, but the separation of the carcasses into their various cuts is done on a different system, particularly in regard to beef and veal, so that it is not easy to get, elsewhere, the precise equivalent of a French shoulder cut of beef for a *pot-au-feu*, of a leg cut for a daube, of a loin of veal for roasting, or escalopes for frying.

PROVENÇAL BEEF and WINE STEW

la daube de bœuf provençale

There must be scores of different recipes for daubes in Provence alone, as well as all those which have been borrowed from Provence by other regions, for a daube of beef is essentially a country housewife's dish. In some daubes the meat is cut up, in others it is cooked in the piece; what goes in apart from the meat is largely a matter of what is available, and the way it is served is again a question of local taste.

This daube is a useful dish for those who have to get a dinner ready when they get home from the office. It can be cooked for 1½ hours the previous evening and finished on the night itself. Provided they have not been overcooked to start with, these beef and wine stews are all the better for a second or even third heating up. The amounts I have given are the smallest quantities in which it is worth cooking such a stew, and will serve four or five people, but of course they can be doubled or even trebled for a large party; if the meat is piled up in layers in a deep pan it will naturally need longer cooking than if it is spread out in a shallow one.

This is an easy recipe, but it has all the rich savor of these slowly cooked wine-flavored stews. The pot to cook it in may be earthenware, cast iron, or a copper oven pot of about 1 quart capacity, wide rather than deep.

> *2lb round of beef, about 6oz pancetta or salt pork, 2 carrots, 2 onions, about 3oz fresh pork rinds, 2 tomatoes, 2 tablespoons olive oil, 2 cloves of garlic, a bouquet of thyme, bay leaf, parsley and a little strip of orange peel, seasoning, 1 cup of red wine.*

Have the meat cut into squares about the size of half a postcard and about ⅓-inch thick. Buy the pancetta or salt pork in the piece and cut it into small cubes.

Peel and slice the carrots; peel and slice the onions. Cut the rinds, which should have scarcely any fat adhering to them and are there to give body as well as savor to the stew, into little squares. Skin and slice the tomatoes.

In the bottom of the pot put the olive oil, then the pancetta, then the vegetables and half the pork rinds. Arrange the meat carefully on top, the slices overlapping each other. Bury the garlic cloves, flattened with a knife, and the bouquet, in the center. Season and cover with the rest of the pork rinds. With the pan uncovered, start the cooking on a moderate heat on top of the stove.

After about 10 minutes, put the wine into another saucepan; bring it to a fast boil; set light to it; rotate the pan so that the flames spread. When they have died down pour the bubbling wine over the meat. Cover the pot with parchment paper or foil, and a well-fitting lid. Transfer to a very slow oven, at 275°F, and leave for 2½ hours.

To serve, arrange the meat with the bacon and the little pieces of rind on a hot dish; pour off some of the fat from the sauce, extract the bouquet, and pour the sauce round the meat. At the serving stage, a *persillade* of finely chopped garlic and parsley, with perhaps an anchovy and a few capers, can be sprinkled over the top. Or pitted black olives can be added to the stew half an hour before the end of the cooking time.

Although in Italy pasta is never served with a meat dish, in Provence it quite often is. The cooked and drained noodles, or whatever pasta you have chosen, are mixed with some of the gravy from the stew, and in this case the fat is not removed from the gravy, because it lubricates the pasta. Sometimes this *macaronade*, as it is called, is served first, to be followed by the meat. Nowadays, since rice has been successfully cultivated in the reclaimed areas of the Camargue, it is also quite usual to find a dish of rice, often flavored with saffron, served with a meat stew.

Enough for four to five people.

SUSSEX STEWED STEAK

This is one of the excellent old English dishes in which mushroom ketchup and ale or stout make a rich-looking and interesting gravy. Creamy mashed potatoes and perhaps a few fried or grilled mushrooms—if you can get large flat ones—go well with this casserole of steak. The whole dish takes scarcely five minutes to prepare for cooking.

> *2½lb of a cheap cut such as chuck steak, top round or thick flank cut in one piece, salt and pepper, a tablespoon or two of flour, an onion, 5 to 6 tablespoons each of port and stout, 2 tablespoons mushroom ketchup or red wine vinegar.*

Season the meat, rub flour on both sides. Put it flat in a shallow baking dish in which it just fits. Over it slice a large onion. Pour in the port, stout, and ketchup or vinegar. Cover with a double sheet of parchment paper and the lid of the dish. Put it in a very low oven, at 275°F, and leave it for about 3 hours—a little less or longer won't matter. The toughest piece of meat emerges beautifully tender, and the gravy rich, bright brown, excellently flavored.

Enough for four people.

BEEF *with* RED WINE, ONIONS *and* MUSHROOMS
bœuf à la bourguignonne

This is a favorite among those carefully composed, slowly cooked dishes which are the domain of French housewives and owner-cooks of modest restaurants rather than of professional chefs. Generally supposed to be of Burgundian origin, *bœuf à la bourguignonne* has long been a nationally popular French dish, and is often referred to, or written down on menus, simply as *"bourguignon."* Such dishes do not, of course, have a rigid formula, each cook interpreting it according to her taste, and the following recipe is just one version. Incidentally, when I helped in a soup kitchen in France many years ago, this was the dish for feast days and holidays.

If more convenient, the first 2 hours' cooking can be done in advance, the stew left to cool and the fat removed; it can then be reheated gently with the bacon, mushrooms and onions added. There are those who maintain that the dish is improved by being heated up a second time; the meat has time to mature, as it were, in the sauce.

To make a cheaper dish, chuck beef may be used instead of round, and an extra 45 minutes' cooking time allowed. And when really small onions are not available it is best simply to cook a chopped onion or two with the stew, and to leave onions out of the garnish, because large ones are not suitable for the purpose.

For formal occasions a boned roast of beef may be cooked whole and served with a similar sauce and garnish, and then becomes *pièce de bœuf à la bourguignonne*.

> *2lb beef round, salt and pepper, a large onion, thyme, parsley and bay leaves, 2 tablespoons olive oil, ⅔ cup red wine, rendered fat from roast beef or butter, 4oz pancetta, a dozen or so small whole onions, 1 tablespoon flour, 1⅓ cups meat stock, preferably veal, a clove of garlic, ½lb small mushrooms.*

Cut the meat into slices about 2½ inches square and ¼-inch thick. Put them into a china or earthenware dish, seasoned with salt and pepper, covered with the large sliced onion, herbs, olive oil and red wine. Leave to marinate for 5–6 hours.

Put a good tablespoon of fat or butter into a heavy stewing-pan of about 2.5 quarts capacity. In this melt the pancetta, cut into ¼-inch-thick match-length strips. Add the whole peeled small onions, and let them brown, turning them over frequently and keeping the heat low. Take out the pancetta when its fat becomes transparent, and remove the onions when they are nicely colored. Set them aside with the pancetta. Now put into the fat the drained and dried pieces of meat and brown them quickly on each side. Sprinkle them with the flour, shaking the pan so that the flour amalgamates with the fat and absorbs it. Pour over the strained marinade. Let it bubble half a minute; add the stock. Put in a clove of garlic and a bouquet of thyme, parsley and bay leaf tied with a thread. Cover the pan with a close-fitting lid and let it barely simmer on top of the stove for about 2 hours.

Now add the pancetta and onions, and the whole mushrooms washed but not peeled and already cooked in butter or fat for a minute or so to rid them of some of their moisture. Cook the stew another half-hour. Remove the bouquet and garlic before serving.

There should be enough for four to six people.

BEEF *and* WINE STEW
with BLACK OLIVES
bœuf à la gardiane

A dish from western Provence and the Camargue demonstrating the stewing of a tough piece of meat in red wine without the addition of any stock or thickening for the sauce.

The old Nîmoise cook who showed me how to make this particular version of the dish used Châteauneuf du Pape to cook it in (we were in the district, so it wasn't so extravagant as it sounds, and it most definitely pays to use a decent and full-bodied wine for these beef stews) and she garnished the dish with heart-shaped croûtons of fried bread instead of rice.

> *2lb top round of beef, butter and olive oil, 4 tablespoons brandy, 1 cup red wine, salt and pepper, a bouquet of thyme, parsley and bay leaf, plus a little strip of orange peel and a crushed clove of garlic, about 1 cup pitted black olives.*

The meat should be cut into small neat cubes, not more than I inch square. Brown them in a mixture of butter and olive oil. Warm the brandy in a soup ladle, pour it over the meat, set light to it, shake the pan until the flames go out. The flaming with brandy, although not absolutely essential, burns up the excess fat and makes quite a difference to the flavor of the finished sauce, which will be a short one, most of the liquid having been absorbed by the meat. Add the red wine; let it bubble fast for about half a minute. Season with only very little salt and pepper, put in the bouquet tied with thread, turn the flame as low as possible, cover the pan with at least two layers of parchment paper or foil and the lid.

Cook as gently as possible, on top of the stove for about 3½ hours. Ten minutes before serving remove the bouquet and put in the pitted black olives. Taste for seasoning before serving. A dish of plain boiled rice can be served separately.

Enough for four or five people.

PAUPIETTES *of* BEEF

*For the stuffing: **2 onions, finely chopped, 2 strips bacon, 6 mushrooms, rendered fat from roast beef or oil, 2 teaspoons finely chopped lemon peel, 1 tablespoon fresh bread crumbs, a handful of parsley, salt and pepper, 1 egg.***

8 thin slices of beef cut from the round, without fat and each weighing approximately 1oz, salt and pepper, thyme, flour, rendered fat from roast beef or oil, 1 clove of garlic, 1 tablespoon Dijon mustard.

Fry the onions, bacon and mushrooms in a little fat or oil, then mix in the lemon peel, bread crumbs, chopped parsley and seasoning, and a beaten egg.

Flatten out each slice of beef; season with salt, pepper and thyme. On each slice lay a little heap of stuffing, roll up the meat and secure with a toothpick, or tie with string. Roll them in flour and brown them in fat or oil, in a small sauté pan. Add water just to cover, and simmer very slowly for 30 minutes. Now with the point of a knife crush a small piece of garlic and add this to the sauce, together with the Dijon mustard, and cook for another 30 minutes. The sauce should be creamy and piquant. The dish can be made beforehand and heated up.

Serve with either boiled rice or a purée of potatoes.

Enough for four people.

SPICED BEEF LOAF

3½lb ground beef, 4oz slab bacon, rind removed, 1 teaspoon each of dried basil and ground allspice, 2 heaped teaspoons salt, 1 dozen peppercorns, 1 very small clove of garlic, ¼ cup port, sherry or red wine, 1 tablespoon wine vinegar.

Put the beef into a big china bowl, add the roughly chopped bacon, all the seasonings and garlic crushed together, the wine and the vinegar. Mix very thoroughly, and if possible leave for a couple of hours so that all the flavors have a chance to penetrate the meat.

Turn the whole mixture into a 1.5–2-quart loaf pan, or two smaller pans. The mixture will shrink during the cooking, so that, initially, the containers should be packed full to the brim. Stand the loaf pans in a shallow baking pan half filled with water and cook uncovered in the center of a slow oven, at 325°F, for 1½ hours.

If the top of the loaf looks like it's getting too brown, cover with buttered foil or parchment paper.

Leave to cool, then store in the refrigerator. To turn the loaf out of its pan simply run a knife round the edges and ease the loaf out onto a dish. Carve it in rather thin slices, and serve with a salad and/or sweet-sour pickled fruits, mild fruit chutney, or a mustardy sauce.

Enough for eight to ten people.

OXTAIL STEWED
with WHITE GRAPES
la queue de bœuf des vignerons

Oxtail "as cooked by the wine growers" is a lovely dish made out of what should be inexpensive ingredients. To make the lengthy cooking worthwhile buy at least 2 oxtails, cut into the usual 2-inch lengths by the butcher, if necessary. A dish of potatoes boiled in their skins, or a potato purée, should accompany the dish.

> *2 oxtails (5–6lb) cut into 2-inch lengths, 3–4oz pancetta bought in one piece, 2 large onions, 4 large carrots, a bouquet of 2 bay leaves, parsley, thyme and 2 crushed cloves of garlic tied in a little bunch, seasonings of salt and freshly ground pepper and a little mace or allspice, 2lb green grapes.*

Steep the oxtails in cold water for a minimum of 2 hours, so that the blood soaks out.

Cut the pancetta into little cubes. Chop the onions and dice the carrots. At the bottom of a heavy cooking pot put the pancetta with the vegetables on top. Start off on a low flame and cook for 10 minutes until the fat from the pancetta is running. Now put in the pieces of oxtail, and put the bouquet in the center. Season the meat. Cover the pot and cook gently for 20 minutes. Pick the grapes off their stems and crush slightly in a bowl. Add them to the pot and cover the pot with two sheets of parchment paper and the lid. Transfer to a very slow oven, at 275°F, and cook for a minimum of 3½ hours. Oxtail varies very much in quality, and sometimes takes a good deal longer, and unless the meat is so soft and tender it is almost falling from the bones it will not be good. Once cooked, quickly transfer the pieces of oxtail and a few of the little bits of pancetta to another terrine or to a serving dish, and keep them hot while you skim off some of the fat from the cooking liquid and then press all the rest of the ingredients through a fine sieve. Pour the resulting sauce over the oxtails.

An alternative method is to cook the dish for half an hour less, take out the oxtails, and leave the sieved sauce separately so that excess fat can be removed from the top when it is cold. Having done this, pour the sauce, warmed, over the meat and heat on top of the stove rather than in the oven, because all-round heat tends to make the sauce oily, whereas with direct heat it will retain its consistency. The dish can, as a matter of fact, be reheated two or three times without damage.

Two oxtails should make six to eight ample helpings.

BRAISED VEAL SHANK

ossi buchi milanese

To make the dish as it should be, very tender veal from an animal not more than three months old should be used. A dish of *Risotto Alla Milanese* (see page 160) always accompanies *ossi buchi*. Incidentally, I have seen it asserted that *ossi buchi* means drunken bones. It doesn't. It means bones with holes, or hollow bones.

> *2lb veal shank (if from a full-grown calf allow 4lb) sawn into pieces 2 inches thick, 4 tablespoons butter, ⅔ cup each of dry white wine and meat stock, ¾lb tomatoes, salt and pepper, parsley, a clove of garlic, a lemon.*

In a wide shallow pan, brown the slices of veal shank in the butter. Once browned, arrange them in the pan so that they remain upright, in order that the marrow in the bone may not fall out as the meat cooks. Pour the white wine over them, let it cook for 10 minutes, then add the skinned and chopped tomatoes; let them reduce; add the stock. Season. Cook over low heat for 1½–2 hours keeping the pan covered for the first hour.

Prepare a handful of chopped parsley, a clove of chopped garlic and the grated peel of half a lemon. The Milanese call this mixture *gremolata*, and it is an essential part of the traditional *ossi buchi milanese*. It is to be sprinkled on the top of the *ossi buchi* before serving.

Enough for four people.

BRAISED MEAT ROLL

polpettone

2lb ground veal, beef or pork, 4 eggs, garlic, an onion, a handful of parsley, salt and pepper, butter.

For the stuffing: 2 hard-boiled eggs, 2oz cooked ham, 2oz provolone or Gruyère cheese, seasoning.

Mix the meat, the eggs, the chopped garlic, onion and parsley together, and season them. Flatten the mixture out on a floured board. In the center put the stuffing of hard-boiled eggs, ham and cheese, all coarsely chopped and seasoned. Roll the meat up into a large sausage. Enclose it in a piece of buttered parchment paper. Melt some butter in an ovenproof dish and cook the *polpettone* in a very slow oven (275°F) or on top of the stove for 1½ hours. If the fat dries up, add a little water or stock, and keep the pan covered. Serve hot but also very good cold. Nowadays I cook this dish in rather the same way as a meat loaf, in a rectangular pan or terrine.

Enough for eight people.

VEAL SCALLOPINI *with* VERMOUTH *and* CREAM SAUCE

escalopes à la savoyarde

It is always difficult to decide what vegetables, if any, should go with this creamy veal dish. On the whole it is best simply to serve a few little croûtons fried in butter, or some small plain boiled potatoes as a garnish, and to keep green vegetables for a separate course.

2 large slices of veal scallopini, each weighing approximately 3½oz, salt and pepper, lemon juice, 1 tablespoon butter, 4 or 5 tablespoons dry white vermouth, ⅓ cup heavy cream.

Season your scallopini with salt, pepper and lemon juice. In a sauté pan, cook them rapidly on each side in foaming butter, pour in the vermouth, and let it bubble. Moderate the heat. Add the cream. Shake the pan so that the cream and wine amalgamate. Now lower the heat again and simmer for another 3 or 4 minutes, until the cream has thickened.

Enough for two people.

LAMB STEWED
with BRANDY *and* GARLIC
tranches de mouton à la poitevine

Have two thick *leg of lamb steaks*, with the bone, weighing about ¾lb each. Brown them in *butter* in a heavy shallow pan with a well-fitting lid. *Salt and pepper* them; pour over about ¼ cup *brandy* and the same amount of water. Add a dozen peeled cloves of *garlic*. Cover with parchment paper and the lid, lower the flame, and cook as slowly as possible for about 45 minutes. There will only be a little concentrated juice when the dish is ready, but the lamb will be very tender with a highly aromatic flavor. You can, of course, use less garlic if you like, but some there must be. Almost any root or dried vegetables go well with this dish, either braised or plain boiled, or in a purée.

Slices of shoulder of lamb can be stewed in the same way, allowing 1¾–2 hours' cooking time.

There should be enough for four people.

SHOULDER *of* LAMB
BAKER'S STYLE
épaule d'agneau boulangère

The boning and rolling of a shoulder of lamb is not really a mystery; any decent butcher will do it for you, and the system certainly does make the roast very simple to carve. This particular way of cooking a boned shoulder owes its name to the fact that it was a dish which would be prepared at home and carried to the bakery to be cooked in the oven after the bread was baked. It makes an excellent and quite economical dish for a large household.

The boned shoulder will weigh about 4lb. Press *salt*, *pepper*, chopped fresh *thyme* or *marjoram*, and for those who like it, *garlic*, into the inside of the rolled meat. People who like the flavor of garlic without wishing to find it in the meat might try putting a clove or two under the roast in the pan while it is cooking. In this way it will flavor the gravy and the potatoes, but will scarcely be perceptible in the meat itself. Personally, I find a little garlic with lamb as indispensable as others find mint sauce.

Melt I tablespoon of *butter* and a tablespoon of *oil* in a large frying pan; brown the seasoned meat in it. Transfer it to a roasting pan; put in the garlic and 2lb of whole *new potatoes*. In the fat in the frying pan fry a sliced *onion* until it turns golden; pour over about 1½ cups of *meat stock*, which can have been made from the bones of the roast, cook a minute or so and pour over the meat and potatoes. Cover with a piece of buttered parchment paper and the lid of the dish. Cook in a slow oven at 325°F, for 2 hours or a little under if you like the meat faintly pink. Before serving, salt the potatoes and sprinkle with more *fresh herbs*. The stock, reduced a little by fast boiling, will serve as a sauce.

Enough for six to eight people.

LAMB *and* EGGPLANT STEW

In countries where eggplants flourish and are cheap, and where meat is scarce and expensive, a dish such as this one would be made with more eggplants and less meat, and the rice would be the really filling element of the meal. It can be cooked in a frying pan or sauté pan, or any wide and shallow utensil of rather large capacity.

Should you have a little lamb stock available—about ⅔ cup—omit the tomatoes and use the stock instead, adding it at the same stage of the cooking. This system makes a dish which has more distinction than the tomato-enriched version.

> *2 small eggplants, salt, 4 tablespoons of oil, 1 large onion, 1½–2lb lamb shoulder boned and cut into 1-inch cubes, fresh or dried mint or basil, pepper, ½lb tomatoes, a clove of garlic and 2 heaped teaspoons of cumin seeds or ground cumin if you prefer.*

Slice the unpeeled eggplants into quarters and then into ½-inch cubes, put them in a colander, sprinkle them with a tablespoon of salt, put a plate and a weight on the top and leave them for at least an hour so that the excess moisture drains out. Before cooking them rinse and press them as dry as you can.

Heat the oil in a heavy 10–12-inch frying or sauté pan and put in the thinly sliced onion. When it has just begun to take color put in the meat, plentifully sprinkled with the herbs, salt and pepper. Turn the meat cubes over and over until they are nicely browned. (If this operation is neglected the dish will be pallid and sad-looking.) Remove the meat and onion to a dish with a draining spoon and into the same oil put the eggplant cubes. Cover the pan and let them cook gently for 10 minutes, giving a stir from time to time.

Now return the meat and onions to the pan, add the skinned and roughly chopped tomatoes, the crushed garlic and the toasted and pounded cumin seeds. Cover the pan again, let it simmer very gently for 1 hour. Or, if it is more convenient, cook it only for 45 minutes and then heat it up very slowly for half an hour the next day. Strew with more mint or basil before serving. Plain boiled rice or pilaf rice goes with this dish.

Ample for four people.

RACK *of* LAMB
with WHITE BEANS
carré d'agneau aux haricots à la bretonne

The *carré* is the French butcher's term for the rack of lamb, consisting of eight chops. It is trimmed exactly as the chops would be if they were to be cut separately for grilling, with the chine bone and most of the fat removed, so that only the actual cutlets with their bones are left. Neatly tied, it makes a compact little roast, very easy to cook and carve, and suitable for a small party when a leg or saddle would be too much.

First of all, prepare a stock from a few *lamb neck bones and trimmings*, with an *onion*, *garlic*, *carrot* and *seasoning*, and water barely to cover. Simmer for an hour or so, strain, leave to cool and skim off the fat. This stock is for basting the rack, so only about a cup is needed. Red wine instead of stock can, if preferred, be used for basting. In this case, pour about 2 cups of *red wine* into a saucepan, add either a couple of chopped *shallots* or 3 or 4 whole cloves of *garlic*, and boil until the wine is reduced by half. Use in the same way as the stock.

Preheat the oven to 375°F. To cook the roast, butter a roasting pan, lay the roast in it fat side up, and cover with a piece of thickly buttered parchment paper or foil. Put a lid on the roasting pan, and put in the center of the preheated oven. After about 20 minutes remove the paper and baste the meat with the juices in the pan and some of the prepared stock, heated. Altogether, the roast will take about 50 minutes to cook and should be basted three or four times, being left uncovered for the last 10 minutes so that the outer coating of fat browns.

When the meat is cooked, keep it hot in a large shallow serving dish. Put the rest of your stock or wine into the roasting pan, scrape up all the juices, let it bubble a minute and add a little of it to the prepared white beans and serve the rest separately.

For the beans: 1½ cups medium-sized and long, rather than round, dried *white beans* are soaked overnight if for lunch, or for 6–8 hours (which is quite long enough provided the beans are those of the current season and not a couple of years old) if for dinner. Drain them, simmer them in water to cover by 2 inches, with a *carrot*, an *onion*, a *bouquet of herbs* and a small rib of *celery*. According to the quality of the beans they may take anything from 1½ to 3 hours. So it is best, if you don't know your beans, to prepare them in advance. They have to be reheated anyhow. When they are tender, but not broken, drain them, reserving the liquid, and season them well with *salt*. Extract the carrot and celery and the herbs and throw them away. Chop another *onion* and fry it in *butter*. Add 3 or 4 skinned and chopped tomatoes and cook till the tomatoes are soft, thinning with a little of the reserved cooking liquid. The beans are gently reheated in this mixture, the juice from the roast being added when they are ready. The beans are then turned into the serving dish round the meat or, if preferred, served in a separate dish. Little paper frills are slipped on to the end of the bones, and the roast is carved straight down into cutlets.

If you like, a Béarnaise Sauce (page 294) can be served with the lamb: in which case you wouldn't really need the gravy as well, except a little to mix with the beans.

It should make ample helpings for four.

PERSIAN LAMB
with EGGPLANTS
maqlub of aubergines

Although this is rather a trouble to make it is one of the best of all eggplant dishes, and the rice, which absorbs some of the flavor of the meat, is particularly good. A good bowl of yogurt can be served with it, and a tomato or green salad.

4–5 medium eggplants, salt, ⅔ cup rice, ½ teaspoon ground allspice, thyme or marjoram, 2 cloves of garlic, ¾lb ground lamb cooked or raw, olive oil, 1 onion, ½ cup blanched almonds, 2 cups meat stock.

Cut the unpeeled eggplants in slices about ¼-inch thick, salt them and leave them for an hour. Put the rice to soak in water for an hour. Mix the allspice, a little thyme or marjoram and chopped garlic with the meat. Rinse and dry the eggplants and fry them lightly in oil, then fry the sliced onion. Put a layer of the fried eggplants in a round flameproof dish; on top put a layer of the meat. Sprinkle with a few sliced blanched almonds and the fried onion. Repeat until all the eggplants and meat are used up, and on top put the drained rice. Pour over half the meat stock, cover the dish and cook over low heat for about 20 minutes. Add the rest of the stock and cook for another 20–30 minutes until the rice is almost cooked.

Put an ovenproof serving dish upside down over the top, turn out the contents and put in the oven at 350°F for another 10–15 minutes. The rice will finish cooking and any liquid left will be absorbed.

Enough for six people. It can be reheated quite successfully, in a covered pan in a gentle oven at 300°F.

ZUCCHINI MOUSSAKA

The more commonly known version of this excellent and useful dish is made with layers of eggplants, ground lamb and tomatoes, all rather highly flavored with onions and spices and herbs, the whole arranged in layers and baked in a pan to make a rich, colorful and rather filling kind of pie. Sometimes zucchini or even potatoes are substituted for the eggplants, and the zucchini version is particularly good.

> *1lb small zucchini, salt, 4 tablespoons olive oil, a large onion, 1lb ground meat which can be lamb or beef, cooked or uncooked, pepper, a teaspoon each of freshly ground allspice and dried or fresh mint, 2 eggs, 1½lb tomatoes, a clove of garlic, 2 or 3 tablespoons each of fresh bread crumbs and meat stock.*

Wash the zucchini but do not peel them. Cut each one lengthwise into slices about 1-inch thick. Salt them slightly and leave them to drain for an hour or so. Shake them dry in a kitchen towel, fry them gently in olive oil until they are tender. When all are done, remove the zucchini, put more oil into the pan and in this fry the finely sliced or chopped onion until it is pale yellow. Put in the meat. If it is already cooked just stir it round until it is amalgamated with the onion. If it is raw meat let it cook gently for about 10 minutes until it is nicely browned. Add seasonings and herbs and, off the heat, stir in the beaten eggs.

In a separate frying pan put the skinned and chopped tomatoes and the crushed garlic clove and simmer until most of the moisture has evaporated. Season with salt and pepper.

Now coat a 1¼–1½-quart square or round, and not too deep, cake pan lightly with oil. Put in a layer of zucchini, then one of meat, then one of tomatoes, and so on until all the ingredients are used up, finishing with a rather thick layer of the tomatoes. On top sprinkle bread crumbs and then moisten with the stock. Cover the pan with a piece of foil. Cook, with the pan on a baking sheet, in a low oven at 350°F, for an hour, but at half-time remove the foil. If the moussaka looks dry add a little more stock. Serve hot.

With the layers of pale green zucchini in between the red and brown of the tomatoes and meat, this is a very beautiful-looking dish, which, provided it has not been overcooked to start with, can quite successfully be reheated.

For a moussaka with eggplants instead of zucchini the proceeding is precisely the same, and you need 2 to 4 eggplants according to size, unpeeled, cut lengthwise into thinnish slices and salted before being fried in oil.

Enough for four to five people.

PORK BAKED
with WINE *and* ORANGES

1 or 2 cloves of garlic, herbs (parsley, marjoram, rosemary), salt and pepper, 4lb bone-in pork loin, boned, with the bones reserved, and the meat tied, a little olive oil, ⅓ cup meat or chicken stock, 3 oranges, 4 tablespoons Madeira, dry white wine or dry vermouth, fresh bread crumbs.

Chop a clove or two of garlic with a little parsley, marjoram, a scrap of rosemary, and salt and pepper. Rub this all over the meat, pressing it well in along the lean side of the roast. Pour a tablespoon of olive oil into a baking dish, put in the meat and all the bones reserved. Let it cook for 10 to 15 minutes in a fairly hot oven at 400°F, before adding the hot stock. Then cook uncovered in a very slow oven at 300°F, for 2½–3 hours.

From time to time baste it with a little of its own liquid. A quarter of an hour before the end of cooking, take out the bones, squeeze the juice of half an orange over the meat and add the wine. Strew the bread crumbs on the fat side of the roast and return it to the oven.

Slice the remaining 2½ oranges into thin rounds, and blanch them for about 3 minutes in boiling water. Drain carefully, and put them in the sauce round the meat for the last 5 minutes of the cooking time.

Serve with sliced oranges all round the meat, and the sauce separately. This dish is even better cold than hot, and if this is how you intend to serve it, cook the sauce for an extra half-hour or so after the meat has been removed, strain it into a bowl, chill it and remove the fat before serving it.

Enough for six to eight people.

PORK COOKED *in* MILK

maiale al latte

3 tablespoons butter, an onion, 1½oz prosciutto, garlic, about 1½lb loin boneless pork, tied, coriander seeds, marjoram, basil or fennel, salt and pepper, 3½ cups of milk.

Melt the butter, brown the finely chopped onion in it, then the prosciutto, also finely chopped.

Stick a clove of garlic inside the rolled meat, together with 3 or 4 coriander seeds and a little marjoram, basil or fennel. Rub it with salt and pepper and brown it in the butter with the onion and ham. In the meantime heat the milk to boiling point in another pan. When the meat has browned pour the milk over it. Add no more salt or pepper. Keep the pan steadily simmering at a moderate pace, uncovered. Gradually a golden web of skin begins to form over the top of the meat while the milk is bubbling away underneath. Don't disturb it until it has been cooking for a good hour. At this moment break the skin and scrape the sides of the pan, stirring it all into the remaining milk, which will be beginning to get thick. In about another 30 minutes the milk should have reduced to about a small cupful, full of all the delicious little bits of bacon and onion, and the meat should be encased in a fine crust formed by the milk, while it is moist and tender inside. It is at this moment that any meat or bird cooked in milk should be carefully watched, for the remaining sauce evaporates with disconcerting rapidity, leaving the meat to stick and burn.

To serve, pour the sauce, with all its grainy little pieces, over the meat. Can be eaten hot or cold. But best cold, I think.

Whatever the weight of the piece of meat to be cooked in this fashion, allow roughly 2½ cups of milk per 1lb. One or two readers have told me they find this recipe very tricky. It can be made easier by transferring the dish, uncovered, to a moderate (350°F) oven, after the web has formed. When the meat is cooked, return the pan to the top of the stove and reduce the sauce.

Enough for six people.

PORK CHOPS BAKED
with AROMATIC HERBS

This dish is a good example of one in which the scent of aromatic herbs makes the whole difference; it should provide ideas for many others of the same sort. If you have time, prepare the pork chops an hour or so in advance, or in the morning for the evening, so that the herbs and seasonings have already scented the meat before cooking starts.

Buy a couple of nice thick *pork chops*. Score the meat lightly on each side. Cut a peeled clove of *garlic* in half and rub the meat with the cut surface. Press in *salt* and a little freshly ground *black pepper*. Coat each side of both chops with *olive oil*. In a baking dish arrange half a dozen sprigs of *thyme*, several whole *bay leaves* and a dozen *fennel* sprigs. On top put the chops. Put the dish under the broiler, and let the chops brown lightly on each side. Now cover the dish with oiled parchment paper or foil and transfer it to a low oven, 325°F, and leave for 40–50 minutes. Finally, pour off any excess fat which has come from the meat during cooking. Serve the chops as they are, in their cooking dish, herbs and all.

A simple enough dish, deliciously flavored; and needing no accompaniment other than a green salad, or a few sliced tomatoes dressed with oil and sprinkled with onion and parsley.

Enough for two people.

GRILLED PORK CHOPS
with CIDER SAUCE
côtes de porc vallée d'auge

Chop 3 or 4 *shallots* very finely with *parsley*; season with *salt* and *pepper*; score 4 *pork chops* lightly on each side and spread with the shallot mixture. Moisten with melted *butter* or *olive oil*, and broil. Have ready a glass of *hard cider* heated in a small pan and when the chops are cooked transfer the broiler pan to the top of the stove; pour in the cider; let it bubble over high heat until it has amalgamated with the juices from the meat and formed a sauce, which will take 2 or 3 minutes. If *Calvados* is available, add a small quantity after the cider has been poured into the pan. It cuts the richness of the pork. Straw potatoes, or a purée, or simply a plain green salad go with the pork chops.

Enough for four people.

PORK NOISETTES *with a* PRUNE *and* CREAM SAUCE

noisettes de porc aux pruneaux

This dish, a speciality of Tours, is a sumptuous one, rich and handsome in appearance as well as in its flavors. But it is not one to try out for the first time on guests, unless you can be sure of ten minutes or so uninterrupted in the kitchen while you make the sauce. Neither is the dish exactly a light one, and is perhaps best eaten, as pork dishes are always supposed to be, at midday rather than in the evening.

Both the utensil for cooking the pork and the dish to serve it in are important. The first should be a shallow and heavy pan to go on top of the stove, either a sauté pan or the kind of dish in which a whole flat fish is poached; failing this the meat will first have to be browned in a frying pan and then transferred to an oven dish. The serving dish should be a big oval one, preferably one which can go for a few minutes into the oven without risk.

> *10oz very fine large juicy prunes (there should be approximately 2 dozen, and the best Californian prunes are perfect for the dish), 1½ cups of wine, which should, by rights, be white Vouvray, 8 boneless pork loin chops, each one weighing about 3oz, seasonings, a little flour, 4 tablespoons butter, a tablespoon red currant jelly, approximately 1⅓ cups heavy cream (you may not use it all but it is as well to have this quantity, as I will explain presently).*

First, put the prunes to steep in a bowl covered with 1⅓ cups of the wine; this is supposed to be done overnight, but with good prunes a half-day will be sufficient. After which, cover them and put them in a very low oven (275°F) to cook. They can stay there an hour or so. They should be quite tender but not mushy, and the wine must not evaporate.

Season the pork very well with freshly ground pepper and salt and sprinkle each noisette with flour. Melt the butter in the pan; put in the meat; let it gently take color on one side and turn it. Keep the heat low, because the butter must not brown. After 10 minutes pour in the remaining 3 tablespoons or so of the white wine. Cover the pan. Cook very gently, covered, on top of the stove, or in the oven if necessary, for approximately 10–15 minutes, but the timing must depend upon the quality of the meat. Test it with a skewer to see if it is tender.

When it is nearly ready, pour the juice from the prunes over the meat—this, of course, must be done over direct heat on top of the stove—and keep the prunes themselves hot in the oven. When the juice has bubbled and reduced a little, transfer the meat to the serving dish and keep it hot.

To the sauce in the pan add the red currant jelly and stir until it has dissolved. Now pour in some of the cream; if the pan is wide enough it will almost instantly start bubbling and thickening; stir it, shake the pan and add a little more cream, and when the sauce is just beginning to get shiny and really thick, pour it over the meat, arrange the prunes all round and serve it quickly. The amount of cream you use depends both on how much juice there was from the prunes and how quickly the sauce has thickened; sometimes it gets too thick too quickly, and a little more cream must be added. In any case there should be enough sauce to cover the meat, but not, of course, the prunes. These are served as they are, not "boned," as the French cooks say.

On the whole, I think it is better to drink red wine than white with this dish. And, of course, you do not serve any vegetables with it. Even with light first- and last-course dishes, 8 noisettes should be enough for four people.

BARBADOS BAKED
and GLAZED HAM

Serve this ham hot with creamed spinach and baked potatoes or a purée of red lentils, or cold with a salad of cubed honeydew melon seasoned with lemon juice and a pinch of ground ginger.

Soak a 4–5-lb piece of *ham* for 12–24 hours in the refrigerator, and preferably for 36, in cold water to cover (and also keep a cloth or dish over the basin). Change the water two or three times. When the time comes to cook the ham, wrap it in two sheets of aluminium foil, twisting the edges together so that the roast is completely enclosed. Stand this parcel on a cake rack placed in a baking pan. Half fill the pan with water—the steam coming from it during cooking helps to keep the ham moist.

Place low down in a very moderate oven, at 325°F, and allow approximately 45 minutes per 1lb. The only attention you have to give it is simply to turn the parcel over at half-time.

Remove from the oven, leave for about 40 minutes, then unwrap the foil, and peel off the rind—this is very easily done while the ham is still hot—and score the fat in diamond shapes. Replace the ham in the rinsed-out baking pan.

Have ready the following mixture: 2 heaped tablespoons *light brown sugar*, 1 teaspoon *Dijon mustard* and ¼ cup *milk*, all stirred together. Pour this mixture over the ham, pressing some of it well down into the fat. If you feel you must, stud the fat with whole *cloves*.

Place the pan near the top of the oven—still at the same temperature—and cook the ham for another 20–35 minutes, basting frequently with the milk and sugar mixture, which will eventually turn into a beautiful dark golden shining glaze.

The sugar, mustard and milk-glaze mixture is by far the most effective, as well as the cheapest and most simple, of any I have ever tried. There really is no need for fanciful additions of rum, orange juice or pineapple chunks.

Keep your cooked ham wrapped in clean parchment or waxed paper, constantly renewed. In this way it will keep sweet and moist down to the last slice.

Enough for eight to ten people.

WINE *in the* KITCHEN

Nobody has ever been able to find out why the English regard a glass of wine added to a soup or stew as a reckless foreign extravagance and at the same time spend pounds on bottled sauces, gravy powders, bouillon cubes, ketchups and artificial flavorings. If every kitchen contained a bottle each of red wine, white wine and inexpensive port for cooking, hundreds of store cupboards could be swept clean forever of the cluttering debris of commercial sauce bottles and all synthetic aids to flavoring. To the basic sum of red, white and port I would add, if possible, brandy, and half a dozen miniature bottles of assorted liqueurs for flavoring sweet dishes and fruit salads, say Kirsch, Apricot Brandy, Grand Marnier, Orange Curaçao, Cointreau and Framboise. Sherry is a good addition, but should be used in cooking with the utmost discretion.

THE COOKING OF WINE

The fundamental fact to remember about the use of wine in cooking is that the wine is cooked. In the process the alcohol is volatilized and what remains is the wonderful flavor which perfumes the dish and fills the kitchen with an aroma of delicious things to come. In any dish which does not require long cooking the wine should be reduced to about half the quantity originally poured in the pan, by the process of very fast boiling. In certain soups, for instance, when the vegetables have been browned and the herbs and spices added, a glass of wine is poured in, the flame turned up, and the wine allowed to bubble fiercely for 2 or 3 minutes; when it starts to look a little syrupy on the bottom of the pan, add the water or stock; this process makes all the difference to the flavor and immediately gives the soup body and color.

When making gravy for a roast, strain off the fat, pour a ½ glass of any wine round the roasting-pan, at the same time scraping up all the juice which has come out of the meat, let it sizzle for a minute or two, add a little water, cook gently another 2 minutes and your gravy is ready.

For a duck, add the juice of an orange and a tablespoon of red currant jelly; for fish which has been grilled add white wine to the butter in the pan, lemon juice and chopped parsley or capers; to the butter in which you have fried veal scallopini add a little red wine or Madeira, let it bubble and then pour in a ½ cup of heavy cream.

TO MARINATE IN WINE

To marinate meat, fish or game is to give it a bath lasting anything between 2 hours and several days in a marinade usually composed of a mixture of wine, herbs, garlic, onions and spices, sometimes with the addition of a little vinegar, olive oil or water. A tough piece of stewing beef is improved by being left several hours in a marinade of red wine; it can then be braised or stewed in the marinade, strained of the vegetables and herbs which, by this time, have become sodden, and fresh ones added.

A leg of lamb can be given a taste approximating to venison by being marinated for several days. It is then carefully dried and roasted, the strained marinade being reduced and used for the sauce. For certain terrines I always marinate the prepared meat or game for 2 or 3 hours in white wine, but red can be used.

THE CHOICE OF THE WINE

There is no hard-and-fast rule as to the use of white or red wine, port or brandy for any particular dish. Generally speaking, of course, red wine is better for meat and game dishes, white for fish, but one can usually be substituted for the other, an exception being *moules marinière*, for which white wine is a necessity, as red turns the whole dish a rather disagreeable blue color, and any essentially white dish, such as a delicate concoction of sole, must have white wine.

from French Country Cooking, *1951*

POULTRY and
GAME BIRDS

The French housewife mixes chopped fresh pork or pure pork sausage meat with eggs and herbs to stuff a big fat fowl, she poaches it with vegetables and a bouquet of herbs and the result is that *poule au pot* which good King Henry of Navarre wished that all his subjects might eat on every Sunday of the year. Or perhaps that same housewife will cook her chicken without a stuffing and serve it with a dish of rice and a cream sauce; or if it is a plump young bird, she will roast it simply in butter and serve it on the familiar long oval dish with a tuft of watercress at each end and the buttery juices in a separate sauceboat. The farmer's wife, faced with an old hen no longer of use for laying, will (if she has inherited her grandmother's recipes and has a proper sense of the fitness of things) bone the bird, stuff it richly with pork and veal and even, perhaps, truffles if it is for a special occasion, and simmer the bird with wine and a calf's foot to make a clear and savory jelly, so that the old hen will be turned into a fine and handsome galantine fit for celebrations and feast days.

If she is in a hurry, the French cook will cut up a roasting chicken into pieces, fry them gently in butter or oil, add stock or wine, perhaps vegetables and little cubes of salt pork as well, and the result will be the *poulet sauté* which, in a restaurant, will be glorified with some classic or regional label, or named after a minister or famous writer or actress. *Parmentier* it will be if there are little bits of potato; *provençale* if there are tomatoes; *chausseur* or *forestière* if there are mushrooms.

Young game birds, pheasant, partridge and grouse (for which the nearest French equivalent is the *coq de bruyère*), are best roasted either on the spit, in the oven or in a heavy pot on top of the stove. The professional chefs, of course, like to do all sorts of elaborate and expensive dishes with them, usually involving truffles and *foie gras*. Pâtés and terrines offer an excellent solution, perhaps the best, to people who have plenty of game at their disposal, while the deep freeze is kinder to game than to vegetables, meat or fish.

CHICKEN *with* TARRAGON

poulet à l'estragon

Tarragon is an herb which has a quite remarkable affinity with chicken, and a *poulet à l'estragon*, made with fresh tarragon, is one of the great treats of the summer. There are any amount of different ways of cooking a tarragon-flavored chicken dish: here is a particularly successful one.

For a plump roasting **chicken** weighing about 3½lb knead 3 tablespoons **butter** with a tablespoon of **tarragon** leaves, half a clove of chopped **garlic**, **salt** and **pepper**. Put this inside the bird, which should be well coated with **olive oil**. Roast the bird lying on its side on a rack in a baking dish. Turn it over at half-time (1¼ hours altogether in a pretty hot oven at 400°F or 1½ hours in a moderate oven at 375°F should be sufficient; those who have a broiler in their oven might try broiling it, which takes about 40 minutes, and gives much more the impression of a spit-roasted bird, but it must be constantly watched and turned over very carefully, so that the legs are as well done as the breast).

When the bird is cooked, heat a few tablespoons of **brandy** in a soup ladle, set light to it, pour it flaming over the chicken and rotate the dish so that the flames spread and continue to burn as long as possible. Return the bird to a low oven at 300°F for 5 minutes, during which time the brandy sauce will mature and lose its raw flavor. At this moment you can, if you like, enrich the sauce with a few spoonfuls of **heavy cream** and, at la Mère Michel's Paris restaurant, from where the recipe originally came, they add **Madeira** to the sauce. Good though this is, it seems to me a needless complication.

Enough for four people.

SAUTÉED CHICKEN *with* OLIVES *and* TOMATOES
poulet sauté aux olives de Provence

The success of all dishes in which the chicken is cut before cooking lies in having presentable portions. Nothing is more dismal than those *poulets sautés* and *fricassées de poulet,* in which all you get on your plate is an unidentifiable and bony little piece from which the dry flesh is detached only with great determination. Some skill is needed to cut a chicken into several pieces and, on the whole, it is more satisfactory to buy smaller chickens and simply split them, or have them split, in half.

One 3½lb chicken, 1 lemon, 1 clove of garlic, a sprig of thyme or basil, flour, olive oil.

Split the chicken in two, as for grilling. Season the halves of chicken, rub them with lemon juice and insert a very small piece of garlic and a little sprig of thyme or basil under the skin of each piece. Dust with flour. In an ordinary heavy frying pan heat 5 tablespoons of olive oil. Make it fairly hot and put in the pieces of chicken skin side down. When they are golden on one side turn them over and, when both sides are seized, turn them over again, turn the heat low and cover the pan, removing the lid only from time to time to turn the chicken. After 25–30 minutes, transfer the chicken and nearly all the oil to a baking dish and put in a very low (275°F) oven, covered, while the sauce is made.

For this have ready: ½ cup of wine, white for preference but red if it is easier, 2 anchovy fillets roughly pounded with 2 cloves of garlic, 4 large ripe tomatoes, skinned and chopped, a sprig each of thyme, marjoram and basil, 4oz pitted black olives.

First pour in the wine, detaching any brown pieces and juices which may have adhered to the pan. Let it bubble and reduce. Add the anchovy and garlic mixture, stir well in, then add the tomatoes and the herbs. Simmer until the sauce is thick, add the olives, let them get hot and taste the sauce for seasoning.

Test the chicken by running a skewer through the thick part of the leg and, if the juices come out white, it is cooked. If still red, leave a little longer in the oven. For serving, arrange the chicken in a long dish on top of the very hot sauce.

Enough for four people.

CHICKEN POT-ROASTED
with FENNEL *and* HAM

Basically, this is a dish of the old-fashioned country cooking of Tuscany. The final blaze of brandy is a modern flourish.

> *A half dozen each of dried fennel stalks and whole bay leaves, a 3½-lb chicken, 2 or 3 garlic cloves, a strip of lemon peel, 4–6oz mild, cooked ham in one piece, a half dozen whole black peppercorns, 4 tablespoons butter, optionally ¼ cup brandy.*

Tie the fennel stalks and bay leaves into a bunch. Put them into an earthenware or cast-iron pot. On top put the chicken (lying on its side) stuffed with the peeled garlic cloves, the strip of lemon peel and the ham cut into finger-thick strips and liberally sprinkled with coarsely crushed black peppercorns (no salt). Add the butter in small pieces. Cover the pot, put it low down into a medium-hot oven, 375°F. Leave for 45 minutes. Now turn the chicken, basting it with the butter, and return it to the oven. Cook for another 50–60 minutes.

Now uncover the pot, turn the chicken breast upwards and leave it to brown in the oven for 10–15 minutes.

To give the dish a spectacular finish, and to bring out to their full extent the scents and flavors of the aromatic herbs, transfer the pot to a mild heat on top of the stove. Pour the brandy into a ladle, warm it, ignite it, pour it flaming over the chicken and rotate the pan so that the flames spread. After they have died down, transfer the chicken to an ovenproof serving dish but leave the juices in the casserole to cook and mature for another 3 or 4 minutes. Pour them off into a sauceboat.

For serving, arrange the fennel stalks and bay leaves on the dish with the chicken. Make sure, when the chicken is carved, that everybody has a share of the little strips of ham from the inside of the bird.

Enough for four people.

CHICKEN BAKED *with* ITALIAN SPICE *and* OLIVE OIL

A really good roasting chicken of approximately 3½lb, 3–4 tablespoons good olive oil, ½ teaspoon of the Italian spice mixture given below, and salt.

For the spice mixture: *3 teaspoons white peppercorns, approximately ½ a small nutmeg, 1 teaspoon juniper berries, ¼ teaspoon whole cloves.*

Put all the spices in a coffee mill and grind them until they are in a powder. The nutmeg takes the longest, and there are moments when the coffee grinder makes a rather angry whine. The quantity makes enough to fill a little glass jar of approximately 1½-oz capacity, and is sufficient to last about 6 months.

Rub the cleaned chicken with salt and paint it with about half the olive oil, then rub in the ½ teaspoon spice mixture. Wrap the chicken in parchment paper or foil, put it on its side in a shallow ovenproof dish. Cook it on the center shelf of a medium-hot oven at 350°F for 30 minutes before unwrapping it, painting it again with olive oil, turning it over onto the other side, re-covering it with the paper, and this time leaving it for 20 minutes. Now turn the chicken breast upwards, use the rest of the olive oil for brushing it over once more, and leave it, again covered, for the final 20 minutes.

Remove the paper or foil carefully so that the juices fall back into the baking dish. Heat them quickly, pour them into a small bowl or sauceboat and use them as the only sauce necessary with the chicken. It will be excellent as a cold dish. Leave it to cool naturally, and serve it with a very simple salad.

The taste of the spice and the olive oil makes a delicate seasoning for the chicken which, given a properly reared bird, will be perfectly cooked, very moist, tender, and the legs still a little pink inside.

The small quantity of olive oil is all that is needed for keeping the chicken moist. All the basting considered necessary with poor-quality birds is quite redundant when you are dealing with a good one. And as for that maddening thing called a bulb baster, I never have understood what anyone could possibly need it for.

Enough for four to six people.

CHICKEN BAKED *with* GREEN PEPPER *and* CINNAMON BUTTER

This recipe also works well with pheasant. For a young bird of about 1¾lb, the timing and temperature are as for the chicken. But the pheasant should be wrapped in well-buttered parchment paper or foil.

For a 3½lb roasting chicken, have ready 3 tablespoons of the spiced butter described below.

Lift the skin of the chicken, rub salt and then the spiced butter well over the flesh, making a few gashes with a small sharp knife in the drumsticks and thick part of the legs so that the spices will penetrate. Put a little more of the butter inside the chicken. If possible leave for an hour or two before cooking.

Put the chicken, with a few *bay leaves*, into a shallow baking dish into which it will just fit. Cook, uncovered, on the center shelf of a moderate oven at 350°F, allowing 25 minutes on each side and 30 minutes breast upwards. Baste with the juices each time the chicken is turned. At the end of the cooking time the skin should be beautifully golden and crisp.

Serve with *lemon quarters* and *watercress*, and the buttery juices poured into a little sauceboat. A simple green salad with a very light dressing is the best accompaniment.

For the green pepper and cinnamon butter, crush 2 teaspoons of drained *green peppercorns* with a small sliver of *garlic* and ½ teaspoon of ground *cinnamon*. Into the mixture work 3 tablespoons of *butter*. When thoroughly amalgamated add a scant teaspoon of *salt*—less if you have used salted butter. Store in a small covered jar in the refrigerator, or make in larger quantities and store in the freezer, keeping a small jar in the refrigerator for current consumption.

Coriander, *ground cumin* and/or *ginger* can be combined with the cinnamon in this recipe, or used instead, and proportions of the spices can be increased or diminished according to taste.

Enough for four people.

DUCK *with* FIGS

Put 16 fresh *figs* to marinate in 1½ cups of *Sauternes* for 24 hours.

Make a stock from *veal bones*, the *giblets of the duck*, 2 sliced *onions*, 2 *carrots*, a clove of crushed *garlic*, and a branch of *thyme* or *marjoram*. Season the duck with *salt* and *pepper* and put a piece of *butter* and a piece of *orange peel* inside the bird. In a deep earthenware terrine with a lid put 4 tablespoons of butter, and put the duck in the terrine, breast downwards, and another 2 tablespoons of butter on top of the duck. Let it brown in a fairly hot oven at 400°F without the lid, for 15 minutes; now pour the butter off, turn the duck over, and pour in the wine from the figs; let this cook 5 minutes and add about 1⅓ cups of the stock. Put the cover on the casserole and cook in a slow oven at 325°F for 1 hour, until the duck is tender.

Now take out the duck, place on a platter, and remove the vegetables and giblets; leave the lid off the casserole, turn the oven up and let the juice bubble for 15 minutes to reduce it; put in the figs, and let them cook 5 minutes if they are the very ripe purple ones, 10 minutes if they are green figs; take them out and arrange them round the duck. Leave the stock to cool. Remove the fat and pour the liquid over the duck and figs; it should set to a light jelly.

Serve the duck at room temperature with a plain green salad.

Enough for three to four people.

WELSH SALT DUCK

This method of salting and cooking a duck is adapted from a Welsh recipe dating back at least a century. (So far as I know, the first time it appeared in print was in Lady Llanover's *Good Cookery* published in 1867.) In the original, the duck was eaten hot, with an onion sauce, which would have been rather heavy, but both the preliminary salting and the slow-cooking methods are worth reviving; they produce a deliciously flavored and tender duck; and the melon goes to perfection with cold duck. It goes without saying that, if you prefer, a salad of sliced oranges more usual with duck can be substituted. Buy and prepare your duck three days in advance.

1 large duck (about 4½lb), ½ cup coarse sea salt, 1 honeydew melon, lemon juice.

Place the duck in a deep dish. Rub it all over with the salt. Repeat this process twice a day for three days. Keep the duck covered, in the refrigerator (use the giblets at once for stock, and the liver for an omelette).

In the morning for the evening cook the duck as follows: first rinse off excess salt; then place the bird in a deep oven-dish. (I use a large oval enamelled casserole, which will stand inside a baking pan.) Cover the duck with cold water, put water also in the outer pan. Transfer the whole contraption to the center of a very low oven, at 300°F, and cook, uncovered, for just 2 hours.

Remove the duck from its liquid (which will probably be rather too salty to use for stock) and leave it to cool.

Serve the duck quite plain and cold, its sole accompaniment the flesh of a honeydew melon cut into small cubes and seasoned only with lemon juice. Baked potatoes could also be served with the duck, but are hardly necessary, and do nothing to help the appreciation of this very delicately flavored bird.

Enough for four people.

DUCK *in* SOUR-SWEET SAUCE

anitra in agrodolce

2 large onions, 4 tablespoons butter, 1 duck weighing 4–5lb, salt and pepper, flour, a pinch of ground cloves, 2 cups chicken stock or water, a little fresh mint, 2 tablespoons sugar, 2 tablespoons wine vinegar.

Slice the onions very thin and melt them in the heated butter. Season the duck with salt and pepper, roll it in flour, and put it to brown with the onions. Add the ground cloves. When the duck is well browned pour over the heated stock or water, cover the pan, and cook gently for 2–3 hours. Turn the duck over from time to time so that it cooks evenly. When it is tender remove it from the pan and keep it warm in the oven. Pour off as much fat as possible from the sauce and stir in the chopped mint (about 2 tablespoons). Have the sugar ready caramelized—that is, heated in a pan with a little water until it turns toffee colored. Stir this into the sauce and add the vinegar. See that the seasoning is right and serve the sauce separately as soon as it has acquired a thick syrup-like consistency. This dish is also excellent cold. Instead of pouring off the fat before adding the mint, sugar and vinegar, make the sauce as directed and remove the fat—it makes the most delicious cooking fat—when the sauce is cold.

Enough for four people.

TURKEY BREASTS
with MARSALA
filetti di tacchino al marsala

Cut 2 boneless *turkey breast halves* (about 1¼lb each) crosswise into 6–8 thick cutlets. Flatten them out a little on a wooden board, season them with *salt* and *pepper*, and dust them very lightly with *flour*. Melt a generous amount of *butter* in a frying pan (if they are all to be done at once you will probably need to keep two pans going at the same time). Cook the fillets on both sides, gently, for the butter must not blacken or burn. When they are nearly done pour over them first about ¼ cup of *Marsala*, and after it has bubbled and amalgamated with the butter the same quantity of chicken stock. Cook in the open pan for another 2 or 3 minutes.

Enough for four to six people.

PHEASANT *with* CREAM, CALVADOS *and* APPLE

faisan à la cauchoise

This is, I think, the best of the many versions of pheasant with apples and Calvados, usually called *faisan normand*. It goes well with a little dish of diced sweet apple, previously fried golden in butter and kept warm in the oven: 2 apples will be sufficient for one pheasant.

Cook a tender roasting **pheasant** in **butter** in a heavy iron or earthenware casserole on top of the stove, turning it over once or twice so that each side is nicely browned. It will take about 40–45 minutes to cook. Carve it, transfer it to the serving dish and keep it warm. Pour off the juices into a shallow pan; let them bubble; pour in about 3 tablespoons of warmed *Calvados* (or *brandy* or *whisky*), set light to it, shake the pan and when the flames have burnt out add a good measure, about 1 cup, of *heavy cream*. Shake the pan, lifting and stirring the cream until it thickens. Season with a very little salt and pepper. Pour the sauce over the pheasant.

Enough for two people.

ROAST PHEASANT
with CHESTNUT SAUCE

A young but fully grown pheasant will weigh about 1½lb and takes approximately 45 minutes to roast.

> For the chestnut sauce, which can be made a day or two in advance and slowly reheated: *½lb chestnuts, 3 tablespoons butter, 2 sticks of celery, one slice of bacon, about 6 tablespoons port, a little stock or heavy cream.*

Put a lump of butter inside the bird, wrap it in well-buttered parchment paper, place it on its side on a rack standing in a baking pan and cook in the center of a preheated fairly hot oven at 375°F.

Turn it over after the first 20 minutes, after another 15 minutes remove the paper and turn the bird breast upwards for the last 10 minutes.

Score the chestnuts on one side, bake them in a moderate oven at 350°F for 15 minutes, shell and skin them. Chop them roughly. Heat the butter, put in the chopped celery and bacon, add the chestnuts, the port, an equal quantity of water, and a very little salt. Cover the saucepan and cook very gently for about 30 minutes until the chestnuts are quite tender. When reheating, enrich the mixture with either a couple of tablespoons of rich meat or game stock or heavy cream.

The mixture is fairly solid, really more like a vegetable dish than a sauce proper, but whatever you like to call it, it goes to perfection with pheasant. A good creamy bread sauce or simply crisp bread crumbs put in a baking pan with a little butter and left in the oven for about 15–20 minutes could provide an alternative, and personally I always like a few fried or baked link sausages with a pheasant.

Enough for two people.

PARTRIDGES BRAISED
in WHITE WINE
perdrix à l'auvergnate

4oz salt pork or pancetta, 4 tablespoons butter, 4 partridges, ⅓ cup brandy,
½ cup dry white wine, ¼ cup white veal or other meat or game stock, a little
bouquet of bay leaf, parsley, thyme and a crushed clove of garlic.

If salt pork is being used, steep it for 1 hour in water. Cut it in small cubes. Put it with 2 tablespoons of the butter in an earthenware or other heavy pan just large enough to hold the four birds. When the fat from the pork or pancetta runs, put in the birds, breast downwards. (If they have been trussed for roasting, take out the wooden skewer before cooking them; it only makes the birds more difficult to fit into the pot and is a nuisance when it comes to serving them.) After 2 or 3 minutes pour in the warmed brandy; set light to it. Shake the pan so that the flames spread. When these die down, put in the white wine, warmed if you are cooking in an earthenware pan. Let it bubble a minute; add the stock and the bouquet. Cover the pan with parchment paper or foil and a well-fitting lid. Transfer to a slow oven, 325°F, and cook for 1½–1¾ hours. Pour off all the liquid into a wide pan, and keep the birds hot in the serving dish. Reduce the liquid by fast boiling to about half its original volume. Off the fire, add the remaining butter and shake the pan until it has melted and given the sauce a slightly glazed appearance. Pour it over the partridges. Serve at the same time a purée of brown lentils or of celeriac and potatoes.

Enough for four people.

PIGEONS *with* PEAS

piccioni coi piselli

A couple of chicken livers, added during the last 5 minutes of cooking, make a good addition to this excellent way of cooking pigeons.

> *1 onion, 2 tablespoons butter, 2oz cooked tongue, 2oz ham or bacon,*
> *2 pigeons, salt and pepper, basil, ½ cup dry white wine, ¼ cup chicken*
> *stock, 2 cups shelled green peas.*

Brown the onion in the melted butter, add the tongue and the ham cut into squares, then the pigeons. Brown them all over. Season with salt, pepper, and basil. Pour the wine over the pigeons, and when it has bubbled a little pour in the stock. Cover the pan and simmer steadily for 1½ hours. Put in the peas and cook until they are tender (about 20 minutes). See that the seasoning is right.

Enough for two people.

PARA NAVIDAD

It is the last day of October. Here in the southeastern corner of Spain the afternoon is hazy and the sun is warm, although not quite what it was a week ago. Then we were eating out-of-doors at midday, and were baked even in our cotton sweaters. The colors of the land are still those of late summer—roan, silver, lilac and ocher. In the soft light the formation of the rock and the ancient terracing of the hills become clearly visible. In the summer the sun on the limestone-white soil dazzles the eyes, and the greens of June obscure the shapes of the ravines and craggy outcroppings. Now there are signs of autumn on the leaves of some of the almond trees. They have turned a frail, transparent auburn, and this morning when I awoke I devoured two of the very first tangerines of the season. In the dawn their scent was piercing and their taste was sharp. During the night it had rained—not much, nothing like enough to affect the parched soil—but all the same there was a sheen on the rose bricks and grey stones of the courtyard. The immense old terra-cotta oil jar in the center was freshly washed, and over the mountains a half-rainbow gave a pretty performance as we drank our breakfast coffee.

At midday we picked small figs, dusty purple and pale jade green. On the skins is a bloom not to be seen on midsummer figs. The taste, too, is quite different. The flesh is a clear garnet red, less rich and more subtle than that of the main-crop fruit, which is of the vernal variety, brilliant green. Some of the figs have split open and are half dried by the sun. In the north we can never taste fruit like this, fruit midway between fresh and dried. It has the same poignancy as the black Valencia grapes still hanging in heavy bunches on the vines. These, too, are in the process of transforming themselves—from fresh grapes to raisins on the stalk as we know them. Here the bunches have been tied up in cotton bags. The two ancients who tend the almond trees (this is Valencia almond country, and it has been a bad season. If the rain fails, next year's crop may prove to be another disaster) and who have known the estate of La Alfarella all their lives, were hoping that the grapes could be cut late and hung in the storeroom until Christmas. Their plans have been foiled by the wasps. This year there has been a fearsome plague of the persistent and destructive brutes. They have bitten their way through the protecting cotton, sucked out the juice of the fruit, and left nothing but husks. Here and there where a bunch has escaped the marauders, we have cut one and brought it back to the house in a basket with the green lemons and some of the wild thyme that has an almost overpowering scent, one that seems to be peculiar to Spanish thyme. It is perhaps fanciful, but it seems to have undertones of aniseed, chamomile, hyssop, lavender.

My English host, who has re-created this property of La Alfarella out of a ruin and is bringing its land back to life after twenty years of neglect, is at the cooking pots. He seizes on the green lemons and grates the skins of two of them into the meat mixture he is stirring up. He throws in a little of the sun-dried thyme and makes us a beguiling dish of *albóndigas*, little rissoles fried

in olive oil. He fries them skillfully and they emerge with a caramel-brown and gold coating reflecting the glaze of the shallow earthenware *sartén*, the frying dish in which they have been cooked and brought to the table. All the cooking here is done in the local earthenware pots. Even the water is boiled in them. They are very thick and sturdy, unglazed on the outside, and are used directly over the gas burner's flame, or sometimes on the wood fire in the open hearth. As yet there is no oven. That is one of next year's projects.

Surprisingly, in an isolated farmhouse in a country believed by so many people to produce the worst and most repetitive food in Europe, our diet has a good deal of variety, and some of the produce is of a very high quality. I have never eaten such delicate and fine-grained pork meat, and the cured fillet, *lomo de cerdo*, is by any standard a luxury worth paying for. The chicken and the rabbit that go into the ritual paella cooked in a vast burnished iron pan (only for paella on a big scale and for the frying of tortillas are metal pans used) over a crackling fire are tender, possessed of their true flavors. We have had little red mullet and fresh *sardines a la plancha*, grilled on primitive round tin grill plates made sizzling hot on the fire. This is the utensil, common to France, Italy, Spain and Greece, that also produces the best toast in the world—brittle and black-barred with the marks of the grill.

To start our midday meal we have, invariably, a tomato and onion salad, a few slices of fresh white cheese, and a dish of olives. The tomatoes are the Mediterranean ridged variety of which I never tire. They are huge, sweet, fleshy, richly red. Here they cut out and discard the central wedge, almost as we core apples, then slice the tomatoes into rough sections. They need no dressing, nothing but salt. With the roughly cut raw onions, sweet as all the vegetables grown in this limestone and clay soil, they make a wonderfully refreshing salad. It has no catchy name. It is just *ensalada*, and it cannot be reproduced without these sweet Spanish onions and Mediterranean tomatoes.

In the summer, seventeen-year-old Juanita asked for empty wine bottles to take to her married sister in the village, who would, she explained, preserve the tomatoes for the winter by slicing them, packing them in bottles, and sealing them with olive oil. They would keep for a year or more, Juanita said. Had her sister a bottle we could try? No. There were only two of last year's vintage left. They were to be kept *para Navidad*, for Christmas.

Yesterday in the market there were fresh dates from Elche, the first of the season. They are rather small, treacle-sticky, and come in tortoiseshell-cat colors: black, acorn brown, peeled-chestnut beige; like the lengths of Barcelona corduroy I have bought in the village shop. Inevitably, we were told that the best dates would not be ready until *Navidad*. That applies to the oranges and the muscatel raisins; and presumably also to the little rosy copper medlars now on sale in the market. They are not yet ripe enough to eat, so I suppose they are to be kept, like Juanita's sister's tomatoes, and the yellow and green Elche melons stored in an *esparto* basket in the house, for *Navidad*. We nibble at the candied melon peel in sugar-frosted and lemon-ice-colored wedges we have bought in the market, and we have already torn open the Christmas-wrapped *mazapan* (it bears the trade name of El Alce, "the elk"; a sad-faced moose with tired hooves and snow on its antlers decorates the paper), which is of a kind I have not before encountered. It is not at all like marzipan. It is very white, in bricks, with a consistency reminiscent of frozen sherbet. It is made of almonds and egg whites, and studded with crystallized fruit. There is the new season's quince cheese, the *carne de membrillo*, which we ought to be keeping to take to England for *Navidad* presents, and with it there is also a peach cheese. How is it that one never hears mention of this beautiful and delicious clear amber sweetmeat?

There are many more Mediterranean treats, cheap treats of autumn, like the newly brined green olives that the people of all olive-growing countries rightly regard as a delicacy. In Rome, one late October, I remember buying new green olives from a woman who was selling them straight from the barrel she had set up at a street corner. That was twelve years ago. I have never forgotten the fresh flavor of the Roman green olives. The manzanilla variety we have bought here come from Andalucía. They are neither green nor black, but purple, rose, lavender and brown, picked at varying stages of maturity, and intended for quick home consumption rather than for export. It is the tasting of familiar products at their point of origin (before they are graded, classified, prinked up, and imprisoned in bottles, tins, jars and packets) that makes them memorable; forever changes their aspect.

By chance, saffron is another commodity that has acquired a new dimension. It was somewhere on the way up to Córdoba that we saw the first purple patches of autumn-flowering saffron crocuses in bloom. On our return we called on Mercedes, the second village girl who works at La Alfarella, to tell her that we were back. Her father was preparing saffron—picking the orange stigmas one by one from the iridescent mauve flowers heaped up in a shoe box by his side and spreading them carefully on a piece of brown paper to dry. The heap of discarded crocus petals made a splash of intense and pure color, shining like a pool of quicksilver in the cavernous shadows of the village living room. Every night, during the six-odd weeks that the season lasts, he prepares a boxful of flowers, so his wife told us. The bundle of saffron that she took out of a battered tin, wrapped in a square of paper, and gave to us must represent a fortnight's work. It is last year's vintage because there is not yet enough of the new season's batch to make a respectable offering. It appears to have lost nothing of its penetrating, quite violently acrid-sweet and pungent scent. It is certainly a handsome present that Mercedes' mother has given us, a rare present, straight from the source, and appropriate for us to take home to England for *Navidad*.

An even better one is the rain. At last, now it is real rain that is falling. The ancients have stopped work for the day, and most of the population of the village is gathered in the café. The day the rain comes the village votes its own fiesta day.

from The Spectator, *27 November 1964*

SAUCES

In simple French household cookery, because they are made freshly and in small quantities, sauces are rather different in both conception and execution from those made by chefs. The first principle is that whenever possible the sauce for a given dish is composed of elements supplied by the main ingredient of that dish itself. That is to say, the trimmings of a roast, the giblets of a bird, the carcass and head of a fish are simmered to make a broth or bouillon which will eventually supply the basis of the sauce. When no such elements are present, as in the case of grilled meat or fish, eggs, vegetables, rice, pasta and so on, then there are the egg and butter sauces of which béarnaise and hollandaise are the two most obvious, and the vegetable purée sauces such as *soubise* (onion), tomato, mushroom. Then there are the sauces of which the juices of the meat or fish itself after it has cooked form the basis, with cream or wine or stock and a binding of egg yolks or flour and butter (*beurre manié*) being used to complete it.

Butter, cream, eggs, wine, olive oil, fresh herbs; these are the ingredients which make the sauces, whether intricate or primitive, for summer food. A few fresh herbs and a little butter or olive oil, or an egg and a lemon, or perhaps a cup of stock and a small amount of cream, well seasoned and carefully mixed, will make little sauces which will turn the salads, vegetables, meat and fish of every day into fresh and original dishes. Fresh butter mixed with chives or parsley or tarragon melting into the juices of a grilled steak is just as delicious in its way as a grand sauce of truffles and Madeira, and more fitting for the summertime. For grilled lamb chops, use mint instead of parsley. Vinaigrette sauces (oil, lemon, herbs) and mayonnaise give plenty of scope to an inventive cook. For example, for a chicken salad add a little grated horseradish to the mayonnaise, or pounded tuna fish and anchovy in the Italian way; blanched and pounded herbs stirred into a mayonnaise make the *sauce verte* which is so good with salmon trout, a beaten white of egg lightens a mayonnaise to serve with salmon.

The foundations of many Italian sauces are olive oil and wine, and they are given consistency with bread crumbs, cheese, tomato paste, pounded herbs and spices. They are simpler to cook than French sauces, there are fewer traps for the unwary: and though they are not so impressive, Italian sauces lack neither variety nor originality, and some of them have great freshness of flavor. Tomato sauce is erroneously supposed to be the unique sauce of the country; it does, of course, play a large part in Italian cookery, but the good cooks use it in only very small quantities, and there are as many ways of making it as there are cooks in Italy. The principles are always the same, but the flavorings and the time taken to cook it determine its character. Perhaps the best are both Neapolitan; *alla marinara*, in which the tomatoes are barely cooked at all, and *alla pizzaiola*, richly flavored with garlic and herbs.

Sugo usually, but not invariably, denotes a meat sauce. The best known is the Bolognese sauce called *ragù* in its native town; but there are plenty of other variations to choose from. The green sauces of Liguria; the basil and cheese pesto, the walnut and parsley sauce for pasta; the fennel, capers, parsley, olives and oil of the sauce for *cappon magro* are aromatic, garlicky, exuberant with all the smells of the Mediterranean.

BÉARNAISE SAUCE

About ⅓ cup dry white wine, 2 tablespoons tarragon vinegar, 2 shallots, black pepper, 8–10 tablespoons butter, 3 or 4 egg yolks, salt, lemon juice, a few leaves of fresh tarragon.

Put the white wine, vinegar, chopped shallots and a little ground black pepper in a small pan and reduce it by fast boiling to about 2 tablespoons. Strain it and add a few drops of cold water. Put this essence in the top half of a double boiler or in a bowl which will fit into the top of an ordinary saucepan. The underneath saucepan should be half full of warm water and put onto a gentle flame. To the liquid already in the top pan, add half the butter, cut into small pieces. Let it melt quickly, then add the rest, stirring all the time. Now add, gradually, the beaten egg yolks and stir very carefully until the sauce thickens. Add salt if necessary, which will depend on whether the butter used is salted or unsalted, and a few drops of lemon juice and a few of cold water. Take the sauce off the heat and stir in the chopped tarragon, and the sauce is ready. At no time should the water underneath the sauce boil and the sauce is not intended to be served hot, but tepid.

Mint instead of tarragon turns béarnaise into *paloise*, a modern variation, useful for serving with lamb.

If you should be obliged to make your béarnaise in advance the least risky way of reheating it is to put the bowl which contains it inside another one containing hot water and stir it for a few seconds, but not over a flame. Never mind if the sauce is not very hot; it is better to have it cool than curdled.

Enough for four people.

HOLLANDAISE SAUCE

Here we get to a vexed question. Purists claim that the one and only true hollandaise sauce should consist of nothing but butter, egg yolks and lemon juice. The truth is that the basic hollandaise is apt to be insipid and many cooks have discovered that the addition of a preliminary reduction of white wine or vinegar, as in a béarnaise, makes a better-flavored sauce. A hollandaise sauce is served with asparagus, artichoke hearts, broccoli, poached salmon, sole and all white fish, chicken, and poached or *mollet* eggs.

In a small pan put 3 tablespoons of *wine vinegar* (I prefer to use white wine if I happen to have a bottle open) and 2 tablespoons of *cold water*. Reduce it by boiling to one scant tablespoon. Add half a tablespoon of *cold water*. Have ready beaten in a bowl 3 large *egg yolks* and, on a warmed plate, 12–14 tablespoons of the finest *unsalted butter*, divided into 6 or 7 portions.

Into the top half of a double boiler or into a china or glass bowl which will equally fit into the bottom half of the double boiler which contains the hot water, put the cooled reduction of vinegar or wine. Add the yolks. Stir thoroughly. Set the whole apparatus over the heat. Add one portion of butter. Stir until it starts to thicken before adding the next portion, and so on until all is used up. Do not allow the water underneath the saucepan to boil and, if you see that the sauce is thickening too quickly, add a few drops of cold water. The finished sauce should coat the back of the spoon. Season with *salt* and a few drops of *lemon juice*.

If all precautions fail and the sauce disintegrates, put another egg yolk into a clean bowl. To this add your failed sauce a little at a time, replace it over the hot water and proceed with greater circumspection this time until it has once more thickened. I should add, perhaps, that this only works if the sauce has separated. If the eggs have got so hot that they have granulated, what you have is scrambled eggs.

These quantities will serve four to six people.

OLIVES
SALÉES
DU PAYS
À VENDRE
HUILE d'OLIVES
de LUCERAM Extra Vierge
OLIVES non traitées
.OLEICULTEUR Producteur.

BÉCHAMEL SAUCE

There are two different versions of this universally known, rather dull but useful sauce. One is a *béchamel grasse*, made with a proportion of meat or chicken stock, the other *béchamel maigre*, in which milk is the only liquid used. The latter is the one more generally useful—in fact essential—to know, for it forms the basis of many others which are infinitely more interesting.

To make a small quantity of straightforward béchamel, first put 1⅓ cups of *milk* to heat in a small saucepan and melt 3 tablespoons of *butter* in another suitably thick saucepan. As soon as the butter starts to foam, add, off the fire, 2 tablespoons of sifted *all-purpose flour*; stir it into the butter immediately. Now add a little of the warmed milk, stirring until a thick paste is formed. Return the saucepan to a low flame and gradually add the rest of the milk. Upon this initial operation depends the success of the sauce, for once the butter, flour and milk are amalgamated and smooth, your sauce is unlikely later to turn lumpy. Having seasoned the mixture with about half a teaspoon of *salt*, a scrap of grated *nutmeg* and a little freshly ground *white pepper*, turn the heat down and let your sauce gently, very gently, simmer for a minimum of 10 minutes, stirring all the time. Half the badly made white sauces one encounters are due to the fact that they are not sufficiently cooked, and so have a crude taste of flour. Also, they are very often made too thick and pasty. A good béchamel should be of a creamy consistency.

After 10 minutes, the saucepan containing the béchamel can be placed in another larger one containing water; this improvised bain-marie is a better system than cooking the sauce in the top half of a double boiler, for by the bain-marie method the sauce is surrounded by heat instead of only cooking over heat, and therefore matures better and more completely.

* If you have to cook your béchamel in advance, cover the surface while the sauce is still hot with minuscule knobs of butter which, in melting, create a film which prevents the formation of a skin.

* Always reheat the sauce by the bain-marie system.

* If the béchamel is to be served straight, without further flavoring, allow a little extra milk and simmer in it for a few minutes a little piece of *onion*, a *bay leaf*, a sprig of *parsley*, a slice of *carrot*, all tied together for easy removal when the milk is added to the sauce.

* If, in spite of all precautions, the sauce has turned lumpy, press it through a fine sieve into a clean saucepan. A blender also comes to the rescue here.

MAYONNAISE

The excellence of a mayonnaise depends upon the quality of the olive oil employed to make it. Use genuine olive oil, heavy but not too fruity, as a mayonnaise always accentuates the flavor of the oil. The more egg yolks used the less tricky the mayonnaise is to make, and the quicker. Lemon juice is better than vinegar to flavor mayonnaise, but in either case there should be very little, as the flavor of the oil and the eggs, not the acid of the lemon or vinegar, should predominate.

In France, a little mustard is usually stirred into the eggs before adding the oil; in Italy only eggs and olive oil are used, and sometimes lemon juice.

It is very difficult to give quantities, owing to the difference in weight of different olive oils, and also because mayonnaise is one of those sauces of which people will eat whatever quantity you put before them.

> *2 egg yolks, salt, about ¾ cup olive oil, the juice of a quarter of a lemon or*
> *a teaspoon of tarragon or white wine vinegar.*

Break the egg yolks into a mortar or heavy china bowl (if you have time, do this an hour before making the mayonnaise; the yolks will be easier to work); stir in a very little salt, and a teaspoon of mustard powder if you like it. Whisk the yolks for a minute; they quickly acquire thickness; then start adding the oil, drop by drop, and pouring if possible from a small jug or bottle with a lip. Whisk all the time, and in a minute or two the mixture will start to acquire the ointment-like appearance of mayonnaise. Add the oil a little faster now, and finally in a slow but steady stream; when half the oil is used up add a squeeze of lemon juice or a drop of vinegar, and go on adding the oil until all is used up; then add a little more lemon juice or vinegar. If the mayonnaise has curdled break another egg yolk into a clean basin, and whisk in the curdled mixture a spoonful at a time. Well-made mayonnaise will keep, even in hot weather, for several days. If you make enough for two or three days, and it does separate, start again with another egg yolk, as if it had curdled.

An average amount for 4 people.

TUNA MAYONNAISE

maionese tonnata

Excellent for all kinds of cold dishes, particularly chicken or hard-boiled eggs, for sandwiches, or for filling raw tomatoes for an hors d'œuvre.

Make a stiff mayonnaise with **2 egg yolks**, *a little* **salt**, *½ cup of* **olive oil**, and *a very little lemon juice*.

Pound or put through a sieve about ⅓ cup canned **tuna fish in oil**. Incorporate the purée gradually into the mayonnaise.

GREEN SAUCE

sauce verte

This is, I think, one of the great achievements of the simpler French cooking, but when I say simple I mean simple in conception rather than in execution, for it is hard work to make in any quantity, and so far as I know there is no short cut.

First prepare a very thick mayonnaise with 2 or even *3* **egg yolks**, 1⅓ cups of best **olive oil**, and a few drops of **wine** or **tarragon vinegar**. The other ingredients are 10 fine **spinach leaves**, 10 sprigs of **watercress**, 4 of **tarragon**, 4 of **parsley**. Pick the leaves of the watercress, tarragon and parsley from the stems. Put all these leaves with the spinach into boiling water for 2 or 3 minutes. Drain, squeeze them quite dry, pound them and put the resulting paste through a fine sieve. It should emerge a compact and dry purée. Stir it gradually into the mayonnaise but leave this final operation as late as possible before the sauce is to be served.

To the salmon of the summer months, lacking the exquisite curdy flesh of the early part of the year, *sauce verte* supplies the interest which might otherwise be lacking, but it need not be confined to fish. A starter of hard-boiled eggs with this green sauce is just that much grander than ordinary eggs with mayonnaise. It never fails to please.

AÏOLI

Aïoli is one of the most famous and most beloved of all Provençal dishes. The magnificent shining golden ointment which is the sauce is often affectionately referred to as the "butter of Provence." With this wonderful sauce are served boiled salt cod, potatoes, beets, sweet peppers, either raw or cooked, carrots, a fine boiled fish such as a porgy or mullet, hard-boiled eggs, sometimes little squid or octopus, green beans, globe artichokes, even little snails and perhaps a salad of chickpeas.

The *aïoli garni* is, in fact, a Friday dish as well as one of the traditional Christmas Eve dishes; on nonfasting days the beef from the *pot-au-feu* or even a boiled chicken may form part of the dish: it then becomes *le grand aïoli*. It will be seen, then, that with all these different accompaniments, the *aïoli garni* is essentially a dish for a large family or a party of intimate friends, although personally I could quite well dispense with all the rest provided there were a large bowl of potatoes boiled in their skins and perhaps some raw peppers and celery to go with the *aïoli*. In a small country restaurant in Provence where I once asked, at short notice, if it were possible to produce an *aïoli garni* for dinner, it was too late for the patron to go out and buy anything specially, but he produced a handsome dish of ham accompanied by potatoes and the vegetables in season, with the *aïoli* in a bowl in the center of the dish. It was an excellent demonstration of the sort of impromptu *aïoli* which can be produced with ingredients to hand.

Allow roughly 2 large cloves of *garlic* per person and, for eight people, *3 egg yolks* and nearly 2⅓ cups of very good-quality *olive oil*—failing Provençal olive oil, the best Italian or Spanish will do. Crush the peeled garlic in a mortar until it is reduced absolutely to pulp. Add the yolks and a pinch of salt. Stir with a wooden spoon or the pestle. When the eggs and garlic are well amalgamated, start adding the oil, very slowly at first, drop by drop, until the *aïoli* begins to thicken. This takes longer than with a straightforward mayonnaise because the garlic has thinned the yolks to a certain extent. When about half the oil has been used, the *aïoli* should be a very thick mass, and the oil can now be added in a slow but steady stream. The sauce gets thicker and thicker, and this is as it should be; a good *aïoli* is practically solid. Add a very little *lemon juice* at the end, and serve the sauce either in the kitchen mortar in which you have made it or piled up in a small salad bowl. Should the *aïoli* separate through the oil having been added too fast, put a fresh yolk into another bowl and gradually add the curdled mixture to it. The *aïoli* then comes back to life.

Now as to the amount of garlic: you can, of course, use less but you are likely to find that the mass of eggs and oil is then too heavy and rich. A true *aïoli* is a remarkable mixture of the smooth mayonnaise combined with the powerful garlic flavor which tingles in your throat as you swallow it.

VERONESE MUSHROOM SAUCE

salsa di funghi alla veronese

In a mixture of **butter** and **olive oil** fry a small chopped **onion**, a handful of chopped **parsley** and a little **garlic**. Sprinkle with a teaspoon of **flour** and then stir in ½lb of **mushrooms**, washed and sliced. Season with **salt** and **pepper**, and simmer until the mushrooms are cooked. The liquid which comes from the mushrooms should be sufficient to amalgamate with the flour and so make a slightly thickened little mushroom stew rather than a sauce. Before serving the sauce, which is excellent for pasta, for chicken, steak or veal, add a generous lump of **butter**.

WALNUT *and* HORSERADISH SAUCE

sauce raifort aux noix

½ cup (2oz) shelled and skinned walnuts, ⅓ cup heavy cream, 2 tablespoons freshly and finely grated horseradish, a teaspoon of sugar, a little salt, the juice of half a lemon.

To skin the walnuts, pour boiling water over them, drain, and rub off the skins as soon as they are cool enough to handle. It is a tedious operation but, having compared the sauce made with unskinned walnuts to the original version, there is no question but that the latter is very much finer. It is an example of how a short cut in cooking can be taken only to the detriment of the final result.

Having skinned the walnuts, then, chop them finely. Stir them very lightly into the cream and add the horseradish. Add the seasonings, and lastly the lemon juice.

TOMATO SAUCE
salsa di pomidoro

Chop 2lb of ripe *tomatoes*. Put them into a saucepan with 1 small *onion*, 1 *carrot*, 1 rib of *celery*, and a little *parsley*, all finely chopped. Add *salt, ground black pepper* and a pinch of *sugar*. Simmer until the tomatoes have turned almost to a purée. Put the sauce through a sieve.

If a concentrated sauce is needed put the purée back in a saucepan and cook it again until the watery part of it has dried up. Before serving it with meat, fish, or any kind of pasta add chopped fresh *basil leaves*.

FRESH TOMATO SAUCE
salsa di pomidoro crudo

Plunge 1lb of very ripe *tomatoes* into boiling water and skin them. Chop them up, adding a little finely cut *onion*, *garlic*, *parsley* or *fresh basil*, and as much good *olive oil* as you care for. Make it an hour or two before it is to be served.

TOMATO, GARLIC and ORANGE SAUCE
sauce catalane

From the Perpignan district, to the west of the Languedoc, where the cookery has a distinct Spanish influence, comes this sauce which in its native region goes particularly with partridges and with pork. But it is good with other things from chicken and lamb to fried eggs or slices of baked ham. The sour orange slices give a curious and interesting flavor to the sauce but do not let them cook in it more than 20 minutes or they will be too bitter.

Heat 2 tablespoons of *olive oil* in a sauté pan. Put in several whole cloves of *garlic* and add immediately about 1lb of ripe, peeled *tomatoes*, roughly cut up. Season with a little *salt*, *pepper* and a lump of *sugar*, and cook for 10 minutes. Now add half a dozen slices of *sour orange*, pips, but not rind, removed. Cook uncovered for another 20 minutes, until the sauce is thick. Remove the garlic before serving.

BANKETTING STUFFE

The flowers we have this month are single anemones, stock gilliflowers, single wall-flowers, primroses, snowdrops, black hellebore, winter aconite, polyanthus; and in the hot-beds the narcissus and the hyacinth.

The Complete English Gardener, *Samuel Cooke, Gardener at Overton, in Wiltshire. London: Printed for J. Cooke, at Shakespear's-Head, in Pater-noster-Row. c.1780.*

That little list of December flowers in the garden at Overton in the eighteenth century reminds me of the delightful directions for garnishing a trifle by Esther Copley in her *Housekeeper's Guide* of 1834. The recipe is a long one, calling for all the ingredients usual at the period—Naples or sponge biscuits, ratafia drops or miniature macaroons, white wine, brandy, split almonds, jam, a pint of rich thick custard, a pint and a half of whipped cream, a scattering of nonpareils (we now call them sugar sprinkles). Having built up the edifice "stick here and there a light delicate flower. Be careful to choose only such as are innocent: violets, heart's-ease, polyanthus, primrose, cowslip, geranium, myrtle, virburnum, jessamine, stock gilliflower, and small roses. These will afford variety, and some of them be in season at most times of the year."

I wonder if the ladies of Overton used some of the innocent flowers, the aconite, the primroses, the polyanthus, grown by Samuel Cooke the gardener to decorate the creams and trifles and custards which surely figured among their desserts at the festive season. How ravishing those eighteenth-century tables must have looked when the crystallized fruit, the oranges and raisins, the spun sugar confections, the trays of syllabubs, the pyramids of jellies, the dishes of little almond cakes shaped into knots and rings and bows, the marchpanes spiked with candied fruit, the curd tarts and all the sweetmeats were spread. No doubt many such delicacies were made in their own stillrooms by the ladies of the household. Others were bought from professional confectioners. Long experience and a specialist's skill were needed—as indeed they still are—to produce the candied and crystallized flowers and fruit, the lemon and orange and citron peel, the sugared almonds, and the gilded marchpane sweetmeats in perfection.

A point which we don't now always grasp when reading of the meals of the seventeenth century is that in those days, the dessert of sweetmeats and marchpanes, fresh and candied fruits, little cakes and biscuits, was known as the bankett or banquet course, and laid out in a room quite apart from the dining hall where the main meal was served. Sometimes there was even a separate building for the banquet room, perhaps in the garden, after the manner of a summer house, or even on the roof. There the party would proceed after dinner, to find the tables spread with "banketting stuffe" as the Elizabethans and early Jacobeans had called the dessert. There would be sweet and spiced wines, the candles would be lit, the musicians would play, and if the banquet room was large enough, there would be dancing.

It was from Italian sources that the English had first learned of the art of sugar confectionery, our early recipes being based on those given in a translation of the French version of an Italian work first published in 1557 by a certain Girolamo Ruscelli, otherwise known as Alexis of Piedmont. This was one of those *Books of Secretes* popular in the sixteenth century, the secrets being at that time mainly medical and cosmetic, and written more for the benefit of professional apothecaries, alchemists and physicians than for the amateur household practitioner. Given, however, the Elizabethan passion for novelty and for knowledge of every kind (the translation appeared in 1558, the year of Elizabeth's accession), it was inevitable that such publications should find their way into many educated households, and the "secrets" be frequently copied out into the recipe books kept by almost every family cultivated enough to read and write.

So it was that the handful of confectionery recipes contained in *The Secretes of the Reverende Maister Alexis of Piedmont, translated out of Frenche into Englishe by Wyllyam Warde* in 1558, reappeared in several little household compilations which found their way into print later in the century. It was a period when sugar was fast replacing honey as the main sweetening and preserving agent for fruit. Everybody wanted to know how to manage sugar, which required different techniques from the old ones used for honey. Alexis of Piedmont dealt with both, which makes his confectionery recipes—there were only a dozen of them—particularly interesting to us, as no doubt also to his original readers.

There were directions for clarifying both honey and sugar, for candying citrons, for candying peaches after the Spanish fashion, for making a conserve or confiture of quinces. There were methods of conserving melon, pumpkin and zucchini rinds in honey, and others for candying green walnuts with spices, cherries preserved in honey, and orange peels also in honey.

Most interesting of all perhaps, to the original readers of the book, were the instructions for making a "paste of sugre, whereof a man maye make all maner of fruites, and other fyne thynges, with theyr forme, as platters, dishes, glasses, cuppes, and such like thynges, wherewith you may furnish a table; and when you have doen, eate them up. A pleasant thing for them that sit at table." The recipe is a detailed one for a sugar paste stiffened with gum tragacanth, but still pliable enough to be shaped into "what things you will" and "with suche fine knackes as maye serve a table, taking heede that there stand no hote thing nigh unto it. At the end of the banket they may eat al and breake the platters, dishes, glasses, cuppes, and all thinges: for this paste is verie delicate and savourous."

From such modest beginnings grew the art of the sugar confectioner, an art which in the Italy of the mid-seventeenth century had already soared to such ambitious heights that the most eminent artists, woodcarvers and sculptors were involved in the design and execution of the ornamental *trionfi*, the triumphs or centerpieces in sugar work made to adorn the feasts given by popes and prelates, princes and noblemen of Rome, Florence, Naples, Mantua, Milan. From Italy this extraordinary art form spread to France, to find its apotheosis in the extravaganza designed by Anthonin Carême, the nineteenth-century chef who is said to have declared that architecture was nothing more than an offshoot of the pastry cook's art.

from Petits Propos Culinaires 3, *November 1979*

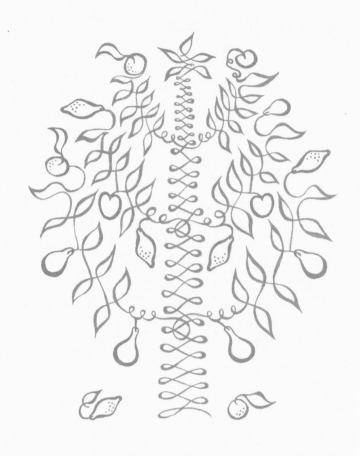

SWEET
DISHES
and CAKES

Please do not look in this chapter for anything but the simplest of creams and cakes, ices and fruit dishes. Elaborate patisserie and confectionery require practical experience and knowledge of an art quite distinct from that of normal household cookery.

The sweet course in southern countries, and particularly in the eastern Mediterranean, frequently consists of very sweet little cakes and pastries, and bowls of fresh fruit. The cakes usually require quantities of eggs, sugar, honey, almonds, pistachio nuts, rosewater, sesame seeds and other *Arabian Nights* ingredients. Very often, little bowls of yogurt are handed round and eaten with sugar and a conserve of quinces or little oranges, more like jam than our compote.

In summer in England there is nothing more delicious than fruit and cream, quite plain when strawberries and raspberries first come into season; later, when they get cheaper, made into fools, purées and pies. Gooseberry fool and gooseberry tart and summer pudding made with raspberries and red currants are among the best things of the English table. Water ices made simply from fruit juice and sugar make a refreshing end to a meal. In the early summer, before the berry season starts, lemons are comparatively cheap and make delicious creams and ices; so do the early imported apricots which are not yet ripe enough for dessert.

In winter in the south there are the succulent dried figs and raisins of Greece and Smyrna; tender little apricots dried with their stones in from Damascus, *loukoúmi* (Turkish Delight) to accompany sweet Turkish coffee. In Italy there is zabaglione, Sicilian cassata and elaborate ice creams. The Spaniards serve nougats and turróns and quince paste with the coffee; the little town of Apt in northern Provence produces delicious candied apricots and other fruits confits, and no one who has seen them will forget the gorgeous displays of crystallized fruits of every conceivable variety in the shops of Nice, Cannes and Genoa.

SUMMER PUDDING

Although nearly everybody knows of this wonderful dessert, authentic recipes for it are rare.

1lb of *raspberries* and ¼lb of *red currants* with about ½ cup of *sugar*. No water. Cook them only 2 or 3 minutes, and leave to cool. Line a fairly deep round dish (a soufflé dish does very well) with slices of one-day-old *white bread* with the crust removed. The bread should be of the thickness usual for sandwiches. The dish must be completely lined, bottom and sides, with no space through which the juice can escape. Fill up with the fruit, but reserve some of the juice. Cover the fruit with a complete layer of bread. On top put a plate which fits exactly inside the dish, and on the plate put a 2–3lb weight. Leave overnight in the refrigerator. When ready to serve turn the pudding out onto a dish (not a completely flat one, or the juice will overflow) and pour over it the reserved juice.

Heavy cream is usually served with summer pudding, but it is almost more delicious without.

Enough for four people.

GOOSEBERRY FOOL

Although this is a traditional English sweet it is not often well made.

Put 1lb of husked green *gooseberries* in a pan with ½ cup of *sugar* (there is no need to top and tail them). Steam them until they are quite soft. Mash them, and when the purée is cold stir in ⅓ cup *heavy cream*, lightly whipped. Add more sugar if the fool is too acid. Serve very cold.

Enough for four people.

RASPBERRY SHORTBREAD

1lb raspberries, a little granulated sugar, 4 tablespoons butter, 1¼ cups all-purpose flour, ½ cup packed light brown sugar, 1 teaspoon baking powder, ½ teaspoon ground ginger.

Put the raspberries in a fairly large shallow pie dish, strew them with the granulated sugar. Cut the butter into very small pieces and crumble it with the flour until it is thoroughly blended. Add the brown sugar, baking powder and ginger. Spread this mixture lightly over the raspberries, and smooth it out evenly, but do not press down. Bake in the center of a medium oven at 350°F, for 25 minutes. Can be served hot or cold and is excellent.

Enough for four people.

RASPBERRY *and* RED CURRANT MOUSSE

½lb each of red currants and raspberries, ½–¾ cup sugar, 2 egg whites.

Sieve the raspberries and red currants—add the sugar and then the stiffly whipped egg whites to the juice. Put into a saucepan over a low flame and whisk continually for about 3 minutes, until the mixture starts to thicken and rise like a soufflé. Pour into wine glasses and serve hot with cream, or into a tall dish in which there is just room for the mousse, and leave to cool. When cold some of the juice will separate and sink to the bottom but can be whipped up again before serving.

A nice sweet for children.

Enough for four people.

MELON STUFFED
with WILD STRAWBERRIES
melon aux fraises des bois

Cut a slice off the thick end of a *cantaloupe* (preferably Charentais or Cavaillon *melon*) and keep it aside. Remove the seeds and scoop out the flesh, taking care not to damage the skin. Cut the flesh into cubes and mix with ¾–1lb of *wild strawberries (fraises des bois)*. Add a little *sugar* and 2 or 3 tablespoons of *port*. Return the mixture to the melon, put back the top slice, surround the melon with plenty of cracked ice and leave for several hours before serving. Do not put it in the refrigerator, as the powerful aroma of melon penetrates all other foodstuffs.

An alternative filling to wild strawberries and port is a mixture of raspberries and Kirsch or Grand Marnier.

Enough for four people.

PEACHES *in* WHITE WINE
pêches au vin blanc

The best *peaches* for this dish are the yellow-fleshed variety. Dip the fruit in boiling water so that the skins can easily be peeled off. Slice them straight into big wine glasses, sprinkle with *sugar* and pour a tablespoon or two of *white wine* into each glass. Don't prepare them too long ahead or the fruit will go mushy.

APPLES *with* LEMON *and* CINNAMON

A cool and fresh sweet dish to serve after a rich or heavy meat course. An alternative flavoring for those who do not care for cinnamon is a vanilla pod, cut in half and put in with the apples before cooking. The lemon slices are still included in the flavoring of the syrup.

Core, peel and slice some good eating *apples*. Put the cores and peel into a saucepan with a scant tablespoon of *sugar* and a slice of *lemon*, peel included, for each apple. Cover amply with water and cook to a syrup. This will take about 7 minutes of rapid boiling.

Put the sliced apples into a skillet, sauté pan, or frying pan. Over them strain the prepared syrup. Cover the pan and cook over moderate heat until the apples are soft but not broken up. Add more sugar if necessary.

Arrange the apples in a shallow serving dish, with a few lemon slices on the top—for decoration and for the scent. These apples can be eaten hot or cold.

An alternative method of cooking this dish, much easier when you are making a large quantity, is to arrange the sliced apples in an oven dish, pour the prepared syrup over them, cover the dish (with foil, if you have no lid) and cook in a moderate oven at 325°–350°F, for 25–35 minutes. Serve the apples in the dish in which they have cooked, not forgetting the final sprinkling of *cinnamon*.

Allow 2 apples per person.

PEARS BAKED *in* RED WINE

poires étuvées au vin rouge

A method of making the most cast iron of cooking pears very delicious.

Peel the *pears*, leaving the stems on. Put them in a tall ovenproof dish, or earthenware crock. Add about ⅓ cup of *sugar* per 1lb of pears. Half cover with *red wine*. Fill to the top with water. Bake in a very slow oven (275°F) for anything between 5 and 7 hours, until the pears are quite tender and the juice greatly reduced. From time to time, as the wine diminishes, turn the pears over.

A big dish of these pears, almost mahogany-colored by the time they are ready, served cold in their remaining juice with cream or creamed rice separately, makes a lovely sweet. The best way to present them is to pile them up in a pyramid, stems uppermost, in a shallow bowl or a compotier on a pedestal.

COFFEE ICE CREAM
glace moka

A luxury ice cream, with a mild but true coffee flavor and a very fine texture.

First put ¼lb of freshly roasted *coffee beans* in a marble mortar. Do not crush them but simply bruise them with the pestle, so that the beans are cracked rather than broken up. Put them in a saucepan with 2⅓ cup of *half-and-half*, 3 *egg yolks* well beaten, a strip of *lemon peel* and ½ cup of packed *light brown sugar*. Cook this mixture over very gentle heat, stirring constantly until it thickens. Take from the heat and go on stirring until it is cool. Strain through a fine sieve. When this cream is quite cold and thick, into it fold ⅔ cup of *heavy cream* lightly whipped with a tablespoon of *granulated sugar*. Freeze in an ice-cream machine. Or turn into a metal pan, cover with foil, and place in the freezer, which should already be turned to maximum freezing point. Freeze for 3 hours; after the first hour stir the ice cream, turning sides to middle. Turn out whole onto a flat dish and cut into four portions.

The coffee beans can be used again for a second batch of ice cream; and a less expensive basic mixture using 2⅓ cups of *milk* and 5 *egg yolks* still makes a very excellent ice. Always use a light roast of coffee.

Enough for four people.

BLACKBERRY WATER ICE

⅔ cup sugar, ⅔ cup water, 2 or 3 sweet-scented geranium leaves (if possible), 1lb blackberries.

Make a syrup by boiling the sugar and water together for 5 or 6 minutes, with 2 sweet-scented geranium leaves, if available. When cool add the syrup to the sieved blackberries, and put into a metal pan with a fresh sweet-scented geranium leaf on the top (or use an ice-cream machine). If using a metal pan cover with foil and freeze for 2½ hours. A tablespoon or two of rosewater makes a fair substitute for the sweet-scented geranium leaves.

Enough for four people.

SNOW CHEESE

This lovely sweet dish is not strictly a cream cheese, but the system on which its confection is based is very similar to the French *crémets*. Recipes for snow cheese occur in English cookery books certainly as far back as the mid-seventeenth century, and possibly earlier. My own recipe is based on one from an early Victorian manuscript.

1⅔ cups heavy cream, ⅔ cup superfine sugar, 1 lemon, 2 egg whites.

Pour the cream into a large bowl; stir in the sugar, the grated peel of the lemon, and its strained juice. Have also ready a round sieve or a cheese mold standing over a plate and lined with a piece of cheesecloth wrung out in cold water.

Whisk the cream mixture until it stands in peaks. Don't overdo it or it will turn to a grainy mess. Fold in the stiffly whipped egg whites. Turn into the lined sieve. Leave to drain in the refrigerator overnight. Turn out onto a shallow dish.

Serve the snow cheese with plain cookies or crisp wafers.

Enough for four people.

APPLES COOKED *in* BUTTER

pommes au beurre

I have never very greatly appreciated cooked apple dishes, but from the French I learned two valuable lessons about them. First, choose hard sweet apples whenever possible instead of the sour cooking variety. And secondly, if the apples are to be eaten hot, cook them in butter instead of in water. The scent of apples cooking in butter is alone more than worth the small extra expense.

For 2lb, then, of peeled and cored *sweet apples*, evenly and rather thinly sliced, melt 4 tablespoons of *butter* in a frying pan. Put in your apples, add 3 or 4 tablespoons of *granulated sugar* (vanilla-flavored if you like) and cook gently until the apples are pale golden and transparent. Turn the slices over very gently, so as not to break them, and, if they are very closely packed, shake the pan rather than stir the apples. Serve them hot; and I doubt if many people will find cream necessary. The delicate butter taste is enough.

Enough for four people.

APRICOT COMPOTE

Apricots are exquisite to eat raw when they are slightly overripe, sun-warmed and straight off the tree. Otherwise they gain by being cooked, and this compote brings out their slightly smoky, delicious flavor.

Halve the apricots and take out the stones. Cook them gently with water halfway to covering them and about ⅔ cup of *sugar* to 2lb of *apricots*. Watch them to see that they do not dissolve into a purée. Take the apricots out of the pan and put them into a dish. Reduce the remaining syrup until it is thick, then pour it over the apricots.

Serve cold. Cream is unnecessary; it would disguise the taste of the apricots.

TORRONE MOLLE

Torrone is the Italian name for all kinds of nougat. This sweet, literally "soft nougat," is an ingenious invention, for it needs no cooking and can be successfully turned out by the least experienced of cooks. The combination of the plain cookies with the chocolate mixture is reminiscent of that most admirable picnic food, a slab of bitter chocolate accompanied by a Petit Beurre biscuit. The *torrone* is infinitely better when prepared the day before it is to be eaten.

> *12 tablespoons butter, 2 cups cocoa, 1½ cups ground almonds, a scant cup of sugar, 1 whole egg and 1 yolk, and plain cookies such as Petit Beurre.*

Work the butter and the cocoa together until you have a soft paste, then stir in the ground almonds. Melt the sugar in a saucepan with a little water over a gentle flame and add it to the cocoa mixture. Stir in the eggs, and finally the cookies cut into almond-sized pieces. This last operation must be performed gently so that the cookies do not crumble. Turn the whole mixture into an oiled rectangular loaf pan or a cake pan with a removable bottom and put it in the refrigerator. Turn it out onto a dish to serve.

Enough for six to eight people.

CHOCOLATE MOUSSE

1oz semisweet or bittersweet chocolate per person, 1 egg per person.

Melt the chocolate in a thick saucepan over a low flame with a tablespoon of water per ounce of chocolate. A tablespoon of rum added will do no harm. Stir the chocolate until it is smooth. Separate the eggs and beat the yolks. Stir the melted chocolate into the yolks.

Whip the whites very stiffly and fold them over and over into the chocolate, so that they are perfectly blended, or the chocolate may sink to the bottom. Put the mousse into a soufflé dish so that the mixture just about comes to the top (nothing is sadder than a small amount of mousse hiding at the bottom of a huge glass bowl) and leave it in a cool place to set. Unless in a hurry, don't refrigerate it, as this tends to make it too hard.

Instead of water, the chocolate can be melted in a tablespoon of black coffee.

CHOCOLATE CHINCHILLA

This is a splendid—and cheap—recipe for using up egg whites left from the making of mayonnaise, béarnaise or other egg yolk–based sauces. It is also a dish which demonstrates the excellent combination of chocolate with cinnamon. This flavoring stems from the sixteenth century, when the Spaniards first shipped the product of the cacao bean from South America to Spain. Chocolate, both drinking and eating versions, spiced with cinnamon is still sometimes to be found in Spain, and also I believe in Mexico, although almost everywhere else cinnamon has long been superseded by vanilla as the favorite aromatic for flavoring chocolate.

Cinnamon varies a good deal in strength. If it has been kept for a long time in your kitchen cupboard, you may find that one heaped teaspoon is not enough to flavor the chocolate.

⅔ cup cocoa, a scant ½ cup superfine sugar, 1 heaped teaspoon ground cinnamon, 5–7 egg whites.

Mix together the cocoa, sugar and cinnamon. Whip the egg whites into stiff peaks. Tip the cocoa and sugar mixture onto the egg whites. Fold the two together, gently but thoroughly. A large metal spoon or a wide flexible spatula are the best implements to use for this operation.

Have ready a buttered ring mold, kugelhopf, or best of all a steamed pudding mold with a central funnel and clip-on lid. Austrian and German cooks use these molds for all puddings and cakes in which there is a high content of whisked egg white. The central funnel helps enormously in the even distribution of heat throughout the mixture, which in a soufflé dish or plain mold tends to remain moist in the center for some minutes after the rest of the pudding is cooked. Whatever mold is used for this recipe, the capacity should be approximately 1 quart.

Having filled your mold with the prepared mixture, stand it, uncovered (for this particular recipe the lid of the mold is not necessary) in a baking pan with water to reach halfway up the dish or mold. Cook the chinchilla—which is really a kind of soufflé without egg yolks—in the center of a moderate oven, 325°F, for about 45 to 50 minutes. It will rise in a spectacular manner. But since it is to be eaten cold, it will sink in an even more spectacular fashion unless, when taken from the oven, it is left to cool in a warm place, protected from drafts and sudden changes of temperature. When cold, the pudding, although shrunk, will have become compact enough to turn out easily. It will have a good texture and a very rich dark color.

Serve with *crème anglaise* to which has been added a little sherry, rum or brandy.

Enough for four to six people.

ST ÉMILION *au* CHOCOLAT

8 tablespoons butter, ⅔ cup sugar, ¾ cup milk, 1 egg yolk, ½lb semisweet chocolate, 12 to 16 amaretti cookies, rum or brandy.

Cream the butter and the sugar until they are well amalgamated. Scald the milk and let it cool, then mix it with the egg yolk. Melt the chocolate, then stir in the milk and egg mixture, then the butter and sugar. Stir this cream carefully until it is absolutely smooth.

In a soufflé dish arrange a layer of cookies, soaked in a little rum or brandy; over these pour a layer of the chocolate cream, then put another layer of cookies and so on until the dish is full, finishing with cookies. Refrigerate for at least 12 hours.

Enough for four to six people.

CHOCOLATE CAKE

gâteau au chocolat

This is a cake which can also be eaten as a pudding, and is neither expensive nor difficult to make.

>*¼lb unsweetened chocolate, 6 tablespoons butter, 2 tablespoons all-purpose flour, ⅔ cup superfine sugar, 5 eggs.*

Melt the chocolate in the oven; mix it with the softened butter, flour, sugar and beaten egg yolks. Fold in the stiffly beaten whites. Turn into a buttered 6-inch cake pan or 3-cup loaf pan and cook in a preheated moderate oven, 350°F, for 35 minutes. There will be a thin crust on top of the cake but if you test it with a skewer the inside will appear insufficiently cooked, which in fact is correct, as it gets firmer as it cools.

As soon as it is cool enough to handle, turn upside down onto a cake rack. When cool, the cake can either be covered with lightly whipped cream or iced with the following mixture. Break up 3oz of *semisweet chocolate* and melt it in an ovenproof bowl in the oven, with 1–2 tablespoons of *sugar* and 2 or 3 tablespoons of water. Stir it smooth; add 2 tablespoons of *butter*. Let it cool, then with an icing spatula cover the whole cake with the chocolate, smoothing it with a knife dipped in water. Leave it to set before serving.

The quantities given make a small cake, but it is somewhat solid and goes quite a long way.

COFFEE CAKE

gâteau moka

This is the simplest sort of old-fashioned plain cake, saved from dryness by a coffee-cream filling, and admirable to serve with creams and ices.

To make the cake, beat a scant ½ cup of *sugar* with 3 *egg yolks* with the seads of ½ *vanilla pod* until the mixture is very creamy. Add ¾ cup of *all-purpose flour* and then fold in the stiffly whipped *whites of the 3 eggs*. Turn into a lightly buttered cake pan (11- by 7-inch) and bake in a moderate oven, 350°F, for about 30 minutes. Turn the cake out upside down onto a cake rack a few minutes after taking it from the oven.

To make the cream filling, work 6 tablespoons of *butter* with 1 *egg yolk*; add ¾ cup of sifted *confectioner's sugar*; when the cream is smooth stir in 2 teaspoons of very strong black *coffee* (nowadays the most convenient method is to use instant coffee powder mixed to a thin paste).

Slice the cake into three or four layers. Spread each liberally with the coffee cream and reshape the cake. Press lightly as you put each layer back, so that the slices will stick together. Leave for some hours before serving.

ORANGE *and* ALMOND CAKE

The juice of 3 oranges, grated zest of 1 orange, 6 tablespoons dry bread crumbs, 1 cup ground almonds or almond meal/flour, orange blossom water, 4 eggs, ⅔ cup sugar, ½ teaspoon salt, heavy cream.

Mix together the orange juice, grated orange zest and bread crumbs, add the ground almonds and, if available, a tablespoon of orange blossom water.

Beat the egg yolks with the sugar and salt until almost white. Add to the first mixture. Fold in the stiffly beaten egg whites. Pour into a square cake pan, buttered and sprinkled with bread crumbs, and bake in a moderate oven at 350°F for about 40 minutes.

When cold turn the cake out and cover the top with whipped cream (about ⅓ cup). Very good and light.

The BAKING *of an* ENGLISH LOAF

Any human being possessed of sufficient gumption to track down a source of fresh yeast—it isn't all that rare—and collected enough to remember to buy at the same time a pound or two of flour, get it home, take a mixing bowl and a measuring cup from the cupboard, and read a few simple instructions can make a decent loaf of bread.

And if you cannot, after two or three attempts, make a better loaf than any to be bought in an English shop—and that goes for health food and whole food and crank-food and home-spun shops generally, just as much as for chain bakeries and grocery stores and small independent bakers—then I am prepared to eat my hat, your hat, and almost anything else put before me, always with the absolute exception of a loaf of English commercial bread.

Please do not jump to conclusions. It is not my intention to make even a slight attempt to persuade you into baking your own bread. I am simply going to tell you how to set about it if you feel you must, and I find it comical as well as shameful that in this day and age anybody should be forced into so archaic an activity.

No Frenchwoman, at least no French townswoman, would dream of baking her own bread. In France, fresh loaves are baked twice daily by every baker and bought twice daily by every householder. If and when the French bakery system breaks down, there is, as every schoolchild knows, a revolution. Had Marie Antoinette been a French princess rather than a Hapsburg from Vienna, she could never have said, or have been credited with saying, that the people of France could make do with cake instead of bread.

As recently as the summer of 1965, the people of Paris rose up in revolt against the annual August closing of some sixty per cent of the city's bakeries. To Parisians, it had become a major grievance to be obliged to walk perhaps as far as a kilometer to find a baker who kept his business open during the summer exodus to the sea and the country. The Government was obliged to step in and decree that the bakers (not, mind you, the shoemakers, the plumbers, the electricians and the laundries, just the bakers) must stagger their holidays. A baker, in other words, has a public responsibility and cannot with impunity desert his post.

In France, a meal without good bread and plenty of it is simply not a meal. For that matter, a meal without bread isn't a meal anywhere in Europe except in England. And I mean England. I do not mean Scotland or Ireland, where it is still possible to buy real bread.

A certain school of English patriot is much given to the expression of belief in the creed that we have in England the finest ingredients in Europe and that "British cuisine at its best is the best in the world." I find it amazing that any responsible person can presume to make such a claim when our basic necessities are so hard to come by, when a new-laid egg is as rare as a flawless ruby, when English butter is not nearly as well made as Dutch, Danish or Polish, when the best fresh vegetables available to Londoners and other city-dwellers are flown from Cyprus or Kenya or sent from Italy, Spain or Madeira, when our cheese is marketed by packaging factories, and when, manifestly, not one householder or one restaurateur in a thousand has grasped the elementary truth that the finest ingredients and the greatest cooking skills this side of Escoffier can combine to produce only a bleak and hollow sham of a meal, joyless and devoid of stimulus, if the customer or the guest is offered no more in the way of bread to go with his food than a skimpy little wedge of white winceyette placed with boarding-house gentility underneath a folded napkin upon a side-plate.

A good many readers of cookery articles must be bored to death with being told that one main dish, with a salad, cheese, and a loaf of crusty bread, makes an ample, balanced, nourishing, economical, easily cooked and satisfying family meal. Well, so it does, if you can get it; in fact, the bread and the cheese would be a perfectly good meal without the so-called main dish. And the bleak truth is that mighty few of us can lay hands on either the cheese or the bread unless we happen to live within walking distance of a specialist cheese shop and a bakery which is not only independent and bakes its own bread but bakes it well and produces it for sale at an hour when the ordinary householder can go out and buy it.

I repeat, I am not canvassing those who are prepared to put up with shop bread because they just have not the time or inclination to make it themselves; I am not preaching to those who buy shop bread because they actually like it; I am giving instructions purely as basic guidance to those who have already reached the conclusion that it is pretty ludicrous to spend three days planning menus to include shrimp-filled avocados, trout with almonds, fillet of beef in puff pastry, pineapple ice cream and no end of a palaver over the grinding and percolating of the coffee, if they cannot offer their guests a decent piece of bread. It should be added, in fairness, that in those households where homemade and well-made bread is on offer nobody needs to worry about all that prestige-type food. Have it by all means, if that's what you like, but if it's prestige you're after—or, to put it in a cruder way and since it isn't unknown to any of us occasionally to do the right things for the wrong reasons—what will most impress your friends and arouse the maximum envy in your rivals is the sight and the taste of fresh, authentic, un-cranky bread, with its slightly rough and open texture, plain unvarnished crust, and perceptibly salty bite.

This is the kind of bread which should be cut in good thick chunky slices straight from the loaf left upon the table for all to see and enjoy.

from Queen, *4 December 1968*

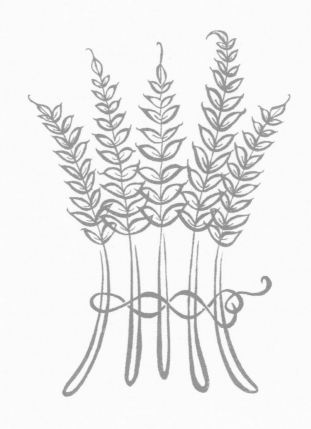

BREAD
and
YEAST
BAKING

The ideal flours for English bread, and for all yeast doughs, are milled from hard wheat, whereas cake, short pastry and sauce flours are or should be soft-wheat flours. Hard flours have a high gluten content, which makes the dough more elastic and expansive. Soft flour tends to make rather flat bread. (French bread is mostly made from a softish flour because this is the type of wheat mainly grown in France. The French have adapted their bread techniques to their flour.) Nearly all the ordinary white flour on sale is soft household flour, but strong white bread flour can now be found on the shelves too. Whole wheat flour, stone-ground, can be bought from supermarkets, grocers and health-food stores and is the whole grain of the wheat with nothing removed and nothing added.

The difference between hard gluten flours and ordinary soft household flours becomes apparent as soon as you start handling the dough. The first almost immediately becomes springy and lithe, the latter tends to be sticky and puttyish, although it becomes harder with kneading.

Flours can be mixed. For example, a mixture of say 1 cup whole wheat flour and 3 cups all-purpose flour make a quite respectable pale brown loaf, although not such a good one as whole wheat and bread flours in the same proportions.

Some of the whole wheat flours on sale in health-food and vegetarian shops make a heavy and pudding-like loaf. For that matter, much of the bread sold in these shops is inexpertly made, dry, heavy, calculated to put all but nut-food nuts right off homemade bread for life. Into the bargain, so-called homemade health food is extortionately expensive.

A BASIC LOAF

This basic recipe is for one large loaf weighing 1½–1¾lb. It is made with a mixture of whole wheat and bread flour—or if you prefer it, all bread flour. The pan should be a 9- by 5- by 3-in loaf pan with a capacity of about 2 quarts.

> *3½ cups bread flour, a heaping ¾ cup whole wheat flour, 2½ teaspoons fine sea salt, 4 packed teaspoons fresh yeast or 2¼ teaspoons active dry yeast, approximately 1½ cups water at tepid blood heat (100°F), and oil or fat for the pan.*

Put the flour and salt into a bowl, mix well, cover the bowl with a heat-resistant plate or dish, and put it in a very low oven (275°) for about 5 to 7 minutes so that the flour is warmed. But not too much so. Leave the plate or dish in the oven.

In the meantime, put the yeast in a cup, pour enough of the tepid water over to just cover it. By the time the flour is warmed the yeast will be soft enough to mix to a cream. If you are using dried yeast you can add a pinch of sugar to the warm water, although with modern yeasts sugar is not necessary. Give the yeast a good 10 minutes to return to active life.

Pour the creamed yeast into the center of the flour. Add some of the tepid water and stir it round with the yeast, using a wooden spoon. Now pour in the rest of the water and mix the dough with your hands. If it is too sticky and wet to work, sprinkle in more flour, until you feel that the dough is becoming lithe and elastic. Work it for a minute or two, until it comes away easily from the sides of the bowl. Form it into a ball, sprinkle it with flour. Cover the bowl with a sheet of plastic wrap and the dish or plate left warming in the oven. By this means both the bowl and the cover are warm, the dough itself generates its own warmth as the yeast works, and unless the weather is very cold it should not be necessary to find a special warm place to leave the dough to rise. If you have no suitable cover for the bowl, use just the sheet of plastic wrap, which helps to generate the damp steamy atmosphere propitious to the dough.

In about 1½ hours the dough will have expanded to more than twice its original volume. It will look puffy and spongy. Break it down by giving it a good punch with your fist. Then gather it up and slap it down hard in the bowl several times. Put the dough on a work surface, sprinkle it with flour and knead it by pushing it out and then folding it over on itself in a roughly three-cornered fashion. The punching down and kneading, or knocking back as it is also called, redistributes the gas bubbles produced by the yeast, helps the gluten to develop and reinvigorates the yeast so that it will renew its work and form new air balloons. With such a small amount of dough, the knocking back and kneading process takes only 3 or 4 minutes. A larger batch obviously takes longer and is harder work, which can be done, if you like, with the dough hook of an electric mixer.

Have ready the warmed pan, greased with a little oil or fat.

Shape the dough, so that the folds are underneath, and put it into the tin. At this stage the amount of dough looks totally inadequate for the size of the pan. But cover it with a sheet of plastic wrap or a damp cloth and leave it in a warm place. Almost immediately it will start coming back to life, and in about 45 minutes—sometimes less, sometimes more—it will have risen to the top of the pan. If the dough has been well kneaded, the second proofing is usually quicker, and the volume achieved greater, than in the initial rising.

Bake the loaf in the center of a good hot oven, 425–450°F, for the first 15 minutes, reducing the heat to 400°F for the next 15. Shake the loaf from the pan, return it, on its side, to the oven, now reduced to about 350°F, and leave it for a final 15–20 minutes. When it is sufficiently baked the loaf gives out a resonant sound when you tap the sides and the bottom crust with your knuckles.

Leave it to cool on a wire rack, or lying across the empty pan. Bread should never be put away until it has cooled completely. As soon as it is wrapped or is put into a container, the crust goes soft, so if I am baking bread in the evening, say for lunch the following day, I leave it uncovered overnight and until it is time to cut it. In this way the crust still retains some crispness.

This type of bread is not good until it is quite cold, and in fact does not develop its full flavor until the day after it is baked.

POTATO BREAD

Usually associated with times of grain shortage, or with a need for strict economy in the kitchen, potato bread is also advocated by some nineteenth-century writers as being the best bread for toast. This is because a proportion of potato mixed with unbleached flour makes a loaf which retains its moisture and is also very light. The pan I use for this loaf is a narrow straight-sided one, as for a sandwich loaf with a capacity of 6 cups. The exact dimensions are not important, the reason for the shape being that I find potato bread makes good sandwiches, as well as good toast, and is also very useful for fried bread.

To 3½ cups unbleached white flour, the proportion of potato is ½ cup very smoothly mashed potato, completely dry, and used while warm. Other ingredients are 4 packed teaspoons fresh yeast, 1¼ cups half milk and half water mixed, a minimum of 2½ teaspoons salt. Note: If you use dried yeast, use 2¼ teaspoons.

Have the flour and salt ready in a bowl, the yeast creamed with a little tepid water, and the additional milk and water warm in a pitcher. When your potatoes (two medium-sized ones will be ample) are cooked, peeled and sieved, mix them with the flour as if you were rubbing in fat for pastry, so that the two are very thoroughly amalgamated. Then add the yeast and the warm milk and water mixture. Mix the dough as for ordinary bread. Leave until it is well risen, which will take rather longer than usual—anything up to 2 hours. Punch it down, knead lightly, shape and put into a greased 8½- by 4½- by 2½-in pan. Cover it with a damp cloth and leave until the dough reaches the top of the pan.

Bake in a moderately hot oven, at 425°F, for about 45 minutes, taking care not to let the crust get too browned or hard.

Notes

1. The covering with a damp cloth while the dough is rising for the second time is important. This dough tends to form a skin, which inhibits the loaf rising when put in the oven, and makes for a tough crust.

2. To cook potatoes to add to bread dough, I find the best way is to boil them in their skins, watch them carefully and, immediately they are cooked but before they start to disintegrate, pour off the water, cover the potatoes with a clean thick cloth, put the lid on the saucepan and leave them for a few minutes. This method produces the best results with indifferent potatoes. They will be easy to peel, and to sieve enough of them to make ½ cup is very quick work, although it is obviously more economical of effort to cook enough potatoes at one go to make potato cakes or potatoes browned in a frying pan.

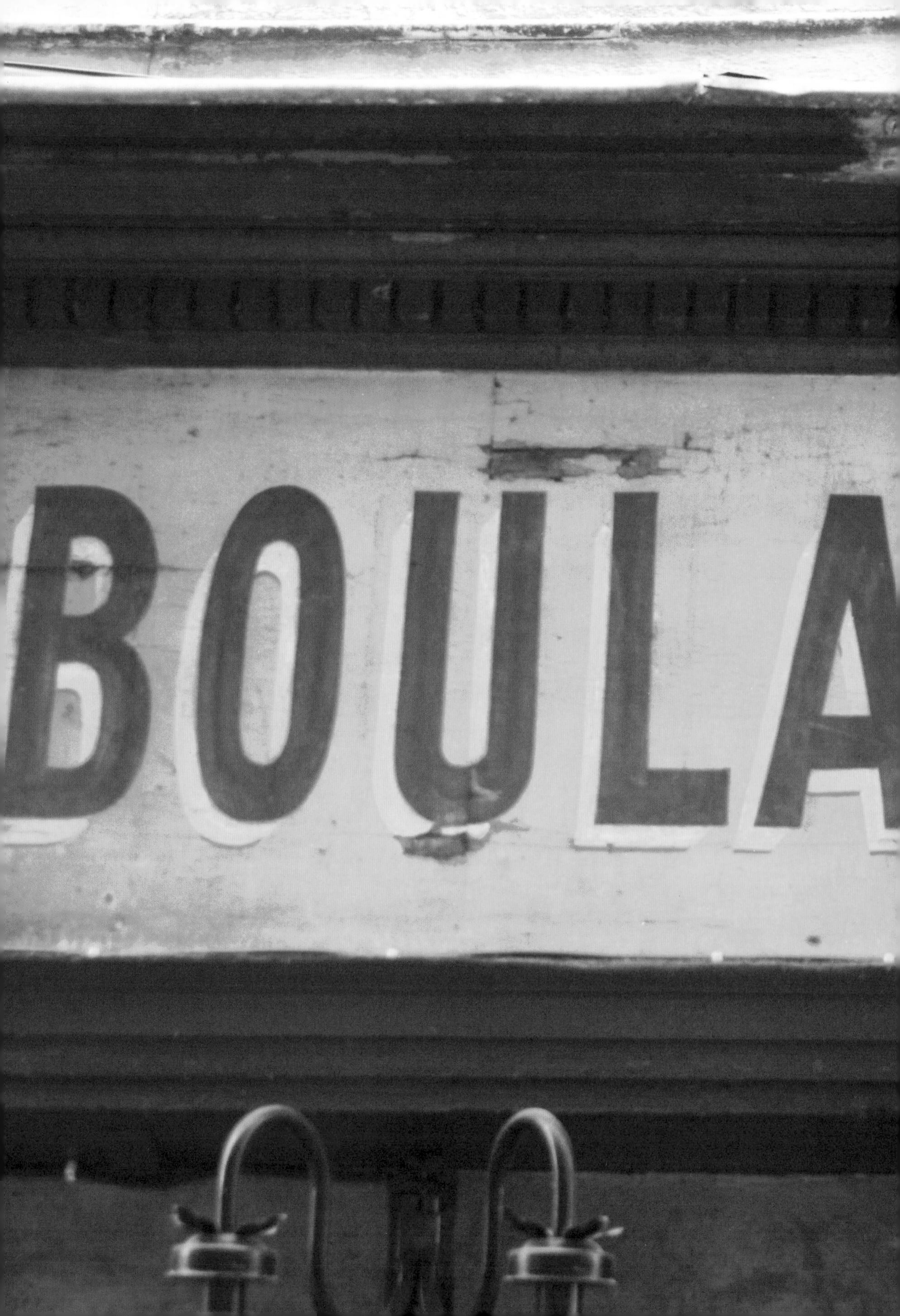
BOULA

NGERIE

RICE BREAD

This is excellent bread for keeping, since the rice remains moist, and the texture is beautifully light and honeycombed. It is also a loaf which is very easy to mix and to bake. The variety of rice used is not, I think, of great importance. I always have Italian round-grained and basmati long-grained rice in the house and have used both for bread. Those who habitually use only brown unpolished rice will know that it takes longer to cook and absorbs more water than white rice. Use a sandwich loaf pan of 8-cup capacity.

About ½ cup uncooked rice, three times its volume of water for cooking it, and for the dough 3½ cups bread flour, 4 packed teaspoons fresh yeast, 2–3 teaspoons salt, about 1⅓ cups water, and fat for the pan. (If you use a larger saucepan you need extra water.) Note: If you use dried yeast, use 2¼ teaspoons.

Put the rice in a thick saucepan of 1 quart capacity, cover it with 1½ cups of water. Bring it to a boil, cover the saucepan, leave the rice to cook steadily until the water is absorbed and little holes have formed all over the surface of the rice.

While the rice is cooking, measure out and prepare all the other ingredients. Cream the yeast with a little warm water. Put the salt in a measuring cup and dissolve it in ⅔ cup of very hot water, then add ⅔ cup cold water.

When the rice is cooked, and while it is still very warm, amalgamate it, very thoroughly, with the flour. Now add the yeast, then the salted water, and mix the dough in the usual way. It will be rather soft. Cover it and leave it to rise for 1–1½ hours, until it is at least double in volume, and bubbly.

Probably the dough will be too soft to handle very much, so it may be necessary to dry it out a little by adding more flour before breaking it down and transferring it—very little kneading is necessary—to a warmed and well-greased pan. The dough should fill the tin by two-thirds. Cover it with a cloth or a sheet of plastic wrap, leave it until it has risen above the top of the pan.

Bake the bread in the usual way, at 450°F for 15 minutes, then at 400°F, for another 15 minutes, before turning the loaf out of its pan and returning it to the oven, on its side, for a final 15–20 minutes at the same temperature. If the crust shows signs of baking too hard and taking too much color, cover the loaf with a large bowl or an inverted oval casserole.

STAFFORDSHIRE OATCAKES

My recipe is adapted slightly from the one supplied by Philip Oakes, writing in the *Sunday Times* in December 1974: it came originally, he said, from the *North Staffordshire Evening Sentinel*:

On Saturday nights my mother used to send me out to buy the oatcakes for Sunday breakfast . . .

> The shop stood half-way down the hill, the bottom of its bow window level with my eyes. It was open for business at 7.30 but always I got there half an hour early to watch the oatcakes being made. Looming above me, his belly bulging in a striped apron, the oatcake man would test the heat of his bakestone—a black iron plate which sent the thermals shimmering to the ceiling—and from a tall white jug he would pour out 12 liquid pats of oatmeal which spat and bubbled on the metal.
>
> There was an instant, mouth-watering smell of toasted oatmeal as the mixture crisped at the edges. One by one, the oatcakes would be flipped over, then with both sides done they would be stacked in a tender, tottering pile beside the bakestone. I would buy 12 and bear them home, clasped to my chest like a hot and fragrant poultice.

When I left the Potteries oatcakes disappeared from my life and the loss was insupportable. I searched everywhere but soon found that they were an intensely local delicacy, unheard of north of Leek, unimagined south of Banbury. Most shops think of oatcake as an oatmeal biscuit. But the oatcakes of my childhood were soft oatmeal pancakes, delicious with butter and honey, delectable with bacon and eggs.

> To make sixteen to eighteen 6–7-inch oatcakes or pancakes: *1⅔ cups coarsely ground oatmeal (whiz in a blender) and bread flour (if you wish, replace 2 tablespoons of the bread flour with whole wheat flour), 2 teaspoons salt, 4 packed teaspoons fresh yeast, approximately 2 cups each warm milk and water. A little fat will be needed for the frying pan.* Note: *If you use dried yeast, use 2¼ teaspoons.*

Put the ground oatmeal and the flour into a bowl with the salt. Cream the yeast with a little of the warm milk and water mixture. Stir it into the flours mixture, add the rest of the liquid and with a wooden spoon beat the mixture into a batter. If it is too thick add a little more warm water. Cover the bowl and leave to rise for an hour or so.

Make the oatcakes as for pancakes. I like them very thin and curling a little at the edges. Oatcakes can be kept warm and soft in a folded cloth; and if you want to make them in advance and reheat them in the pan or in a slow (300°F) oven, dampen the cloth so that they remain moist.

Enough for eight or nine people.

THICK PARMESAN BISCUITS

A little-known recipe from *The Cookery Book of Lady Clark of Tillypronie*, compiled from a treasure-house of notebooks left by Lady Clark and published in 1909, nine years after her death. As is inevitable in books compiled from cookery notebooks, Lady Clark's recipes are often sketchy. It is for the ideas, the historical aspect and the feeling of authenticity, the certainty that these recipes were actually used and the dishes successful—or they would not have been recorded—that the book is so valuable.

This recipe is an exceptionally good one. With the help of a friend, I once made a huge batch of them for an Anglo-Greek wedding party held in my London house. Smoked salmon and chicken sandwiches made with the home-baked bread of the house, and an immense pyramid of the delicate Greek shortbread cakes called *kourabiedes* made by the bridegroom's mother, Greek sugared almonds, and an English cake (bought) completed a quite notable although extremely simple wedding buffet.

> *4 tablespoons butter, a generous ¾ cup all-purpose flour, ¼ cup grated Parmesan, 1 egg yolk, salt, cayenne pepper.*

Rub the butter into the flour, add the cheese, egg and seasonings. Moisten with a little water if necessary. Roll out the dough to the thickness of ½ inch. Cut into 1-inch diameter rounds. Arrange on a baking sheet. Bake in the center or lower third of a very moderate oven, at 300°F, for just about 20 minutes. Serve hot.

Lady Clark makes the point that it is the thickness of these biscuits that gives them their character. The Parmesan is also essential. English cheese will not do.

The biscuits can be stored in a tin and heated up when wanted.

Makes 12 biscuits.

The ITALIAN PIZZA and the FRENCH PISSALADIÈRE

In colloquial Italian the word "pizza" denotes a pie of almost any kind, savory or sweet, open or covered, and with a basis of any variety of pastry or of leavened dough, and to the English-speaking world a pizza means a flat, round, open pie with a filling of tomato and onion topped with melting cheese.

In short, the pizza which has travelled the world, reached almost every deep-freezer in Europe and America, become a mainstay of the take-out shops, and is manufactured by the ton in the food-processing factories, was originally the Neapolitan interpretation of an ancient method of dealing with a piece of bread dough in a rough and ready fashion, strewing it with a few onions, a handful of salt sardines or anchovies, or a sprinkling of pork cracklings left from the rendering down of lard. To us the pizza may be indissolubly associated with the tomato, but it did of course exist long before tomatoes were cultivated in Europe. Something like it was familiar to the Greeks and to the Romans, probably the early Arabs had a version of it—they certainly have one now—and the Armenians claim that they invented it (perhaps they did); there are variations to be found in Spain where it is called *coca*, meaning a kind of cake, and in Provence where it was once known as *pissaladeira*, and has now all but merged with the universal pizza. In eastern France the quiche of Lorraine, almost as much a victim of current fashion and factory production as the pizza, was originally made on a basis of bread dough, and a quiche was not committed exclusively to a filling of bacon and cream and eggs. It could be, and often was, the basis for a spread of fresh plums or cherries, which baked to a delicious sticky, sugary mass. This brings it all nearer home, to our own lardy cakes and fruit-enriched doughs. For surely, anywhere there was leavened bread there was likely to be left-over dough, to be quickly made up and baked to provide something cheap and filling for children, for the poor, the hungry.

What seems extraordinary is that so many people in so many places can be induced into paying so high a price for something so simple and cheap to make at home and so difficult to reproduce in mass-market terms as the Neapolitan pizza. Even taking into consideration your own time and work plus the cost of the oven fuel, a homemade pizza is something of a bargain, making the mass-produced "pizza pie"—many are made with a baking powder dough, not a yeast-leavened one, hence their incredible toughness—seem rather more of a confidence trick than most products of its kind. This is probably because being an alien import with an unfamiliar name it contains a built-in mystique. Equivalent prices for a hot cheese sandwich or a take-out portion of cottage pie would soon meet with resistance.

Now, it must be said that the authentic Neapolitan pizza was—and is—heavy-going, and lies uneasy on any but the most robust of stomachs. It became popular because it was cheap, and the original pizzeria, or pizza house, furnished with its own brick oven in which every pizza was baked to order, was a refuge—if rather a noisy one—where the hungry and hard-up could eat their hefty round of cheese-topped pizza and drink a glass or two of cheap wine for the equivalent of a few pence. As late as 1950 the pizzeria was an almost exclusively southern Italian institution. The beehive-shaped brick oven installed in the pizzeria was a conscious survival, or revival, of the ancient, traditional bread oven, and it was then rare to find a pizzeria north of Rome, whereas now there must be one or more in almost every town throughout the Italian peninsula.

Along the Mediterranean coast, west beyond Genoa and across the borders of Provence a different version of pizza was to be bought from the bakeries. It was baked and displayed for sale in huge rectangular iron oven trays from which the customers could buy slices at the same time as they bought their morning bread. On the Ligurian coast this pizza was known as a sardenara, because originally salted sardines were part of the top dressing, the basis of which was onion and tomato. In Provence between Nice and Marseilles the *pissaladeira*, very similar to the *sardenara*, owed its name to *pissala*, a brined and potted mixture of small-fry peculiar to the coasts of the County of Nice and of Provence. By the time I first encountered the *pissaladeira*, in the 1930s, anchovies had taken the place of the *pissala*, and there were basically two kinds of dressings for the bread dough, one mainly of onions stewed in olive oil, with black olives added, the other with tomatoes, anchovies and, again, black olives. A third, called *anchoïade*, was an anchovy and garlic mixture. This one is now nearly always made on a basis of previously cooked, fresh and thick bread slices, but is much nicer spread on the raw dough and then baked. None of these versions featured the cheese of the Neapolitan pizza.

These variations, then, are the ones upon which I base my own pizza mixtures: onion, tomato, anchovy, black olives, in varying proportions and not necessarily all at once, but always cooked in olive oil and flavored with oregano, the wild marjoram of Italy. Sometimes, but not invariably, garlic goes into the mixture. I don't include any top dressing of chewy cheese. The pizza manufacturers, evidently believing it to be an essential selling point, use either processed Cheddar or a specially developed "pizza Mozzarella." Both seem to me quite pointless. The mass-market product would be better as well as cheaper without them.

The dough I use is what the Italians would call *casalinga*, a household dough rather than a baker's basic bread dough, which means it is made rather lighter, with an egg or two and olive oil—or butter if you prefer it—so that what it amounts to is a very modified form of brioche dough.

Once you have acquired the knack of making this dough—it was through the pizza that I first discovered how easy it is to work with yeast—it is no trouble whatever to make a pizza in any size or form you please.

One word of advice, though, as to the filling or dressing for the dough. A great many English people make the mistake of thinking that the more oddments added in the way of bits of sausage, bacon, mushrooms, shrimp and anything else that comes to hand, the better the pizza will be. In fact the reverse is true. The black olives for example, can be eliminated but you can use a few extra anchovies. And tomato is not obligatory any more than is cheese. Just onions, if you like them, slowly, slowly stewed in olive oil, and with a final addition of anchovy fillets before the dough goes into the oven, make an excellent pizza. For those allergic to onions, a tomato filling without them is perfectly feasible. There is really no problem and not many rules. The idea is, basically, that what you spread on the dough sinks into it, amalgamates itself with, and becomes an integral part of, the bread as it bakes. A mass of bitty things won't do this. They will just stay on top of the dough, toughen and probably burn as the pizza cooks. It is insufficient understanding of the nature and behavior of leavened dough which causes English cooks to attempt so many nonviable additions and substitutions. Or is it the English propensity for treating every basic dish, so long as it is a foreign one, as a dustbin for the reception of leftovers?

from English Bread and Yeast Cookery, *1977*

LIGURIAN PIZZA
sardenara

This recipe is for a small pizza baked in an 8-inch shallow tart pan with a removable base. For those unfamiliar with yeast-leavened dough and its workings, this is the easiest way to start, and the best way to ensure that a presentable pizza will be produced at the first attempt.

For the dough: *2 packed teaspoons fresh yeast, 3 tablespoons warm milk, ½ teaspoon salt, 1 cup unbleached or bread flour, 1 whole egg, 2 tablespoons olive oil.* Note: *If you use active dry yeast, use 1¼ teaspoons.*

For the filling: *1lb ripe tomatoes, or half and half fresh and Italian canned tomatoes, 2 small onions, 2 cloves of garlic, salt, sugar, freshly ground pepper, dried oregano, olive oil, 2oz can of flat anchovy fillets in olive oil, 12 very small black olives with their pits removed.*

To make the dough: put the yeast into a cup with the milk. Mix it to a cream. Put the flour into a bowl with the salt, warm it for 4 or 5 minutes—no longer—in a very low (275°F) oven; add the yeast mixture, then the whole egg and the olive oil. Mix all well together, then with your hands knead the dough for five minutes until it is smooth. Form it into a ball. Shake a little extra flour over it. Cover the bowl. Put it in a warm place and leave for 1½–2 hours until the dough is well risen and very light.

To make the filling: pour boiling water over the tomatoes, leave them a couple of minutes, then slip off the skins. Chop the tomatoes roughly. Peel the onions, slice them into the thinnest possible rounds. Peel the garlic cloves. Crush them with the flat of a knife. Into a heavy 10-inch frying pan or sauté pan put enough olive oil to cover the surface. Let the oil warm over low heat then put in the onions. They should stew gently, without frying, for about 7 minutes. Add the crushed garlic cloves, then the fresh tomatoes. With the pan uncovered, increase the heat, so that the water content of the tomatoes evaporates rapidly. Add seasonings of salt and a very little sugar. When the fresh tomatoes have reduced almost to a pulp add the canned ones if you are using them. There is no need to chop them. Simply spoon them into the pan with some of their juice and crush them with a wooden spoon.

Cook for a further few minutes, until the sauce has again reduced. Taste for seasoning—not forgetting that the olives and anchovies will provide extra salt—and scatter in a scant teaspoon of oregano. The basis of the pizza filling is now ready. The olives and anchovies are added when the dough is spread with the tomato mixture and is all but ready to cook.

Brush the tart pan, or a round iron sheet with slightly raised rim, or an earthenware plate of similar shape and size, with olive oil. Punch down the dough, which should have doubled in volume and feel puffy and soft, sprinkle it with flour so that it does not stick to your hands, reshape it into a ball which you put into the center of the oiled pan. With your knuckles gently press out the dough until it fills the pan. Turn the oven on to fairly hot, 425°–450°F, and have a baking sheet ready on the center shelf.

Now spread the dough with the warm tomato mixture, break the anchovy fillets into pieces and arrange them at random on the top. Season them with a little ground black pepper. Scatter the black olives among the pieces of anchovy, add a final extra sprinkling of oregano and olive oil.

Leave the prepared pizza on the top of the stove for about 10 minutes, until the oven is really hot and the dough has started to rise again. Now slip the pan into the oven, leave it for 15 minutes, then decrease the heat to 375°F, and cook for another 10–15 minutes. Alternatively, leave the oven at the same temperature and simply move the pizza to a lower shelf. If the filling begins to look dry, cover it with a piece of oiled foil or parchment paper.

Serve your pizza hot, with the base of the tart pan still underneath it, the whole on a flat serving platter.

Enough for four people for a first course.

A LARGE ROUND PIZZA *in the* MIDDLE EASTERN MANNER

The filling for this pizza is made with meat, spices, garlic and a good deal of tomato. In Armenian and Lebanese cooking the ground berries of a plant called sumac are much used as a spice and should go into the filling. Sumac can be found in some Middle Eastern shops. It is because, for most of us, the filling must be made without this spice that I call it "in the Middle Eastern manner." This is an excellent pizza, in some ways the best of all, and if you have lamb left from a roast it provides a splendid way of using it, and at very little cost.

For the dough: *2½ packed teaspoons fresh yeast, approximately ⅔ cup warm milk, 2¼ cups bread flour, 1 teaspoon salt, 1 whole large egg, 2 tablespoons olive oil. More olive oil will be needed for the dish.* Note: *If you use active dry yeast, use 1½ teaspoons.*

For the filling: *a small onion, olive oil, 8oz cooked or raw ground lamb, 2 or 3 cloves of garlic, salt, seasonings of ground cinnamon, cumin, cloves, pepper and sumac(if available), 1 cup canned tomatoes, 1 teaspoon sugar, 1 teaspoon dried mint.*

To cook the filling, melt the chopped onion in olive oil. Add the meat and let it brown gently; put in the peeled and crushed garlic cloves, salt, a level teaspoon each of cinnamon and ground cumin, a half teaspoon of ground cloves, and the same of freshly ground black pepper and sumac. Add the tomatoes, cover the pan and simmer gently until the juice has evaporated and the whole mixture is fairly thick. Taste it for seasoning. It should be really well spiced, so may need more pepper and perhaps extra cumin. A teaspoon or two of sugar may be needed, and a little dried mint can also be added.

Having mixed the dough (as on page 366) and left it to rise until very light and puffy, oil a large 12-inch platter and spread the dough on it, taking it right up to the edges. Leave it, covered, for 15 minutes, until it has returned to life. Spread the warm filling over it. There should not be too thick a layer. Again leave the prepared pizza for 10–15 minutes before putting it into the oven at 450°F for 15 minutes. In either case it is a good idea to cover the pizza with a piece of oiled parchment paper at half time, as the filling should not dry out.

Enough for seven to ten people for a first course.

PROVENÇAL ONION PIE
pissaladière

Pissaladière is not so common nowadays as it was before the war, when it could be bought hot from the oven in the early morning at every street corner in the old quarters of Marseille and Toulon. Not so long ago, however, having spotted some in a bakery in Avignon, I went in and asked for *'une tranche de Pissaladière'*. The shopkeeper did not know what I meant. 'What, then, is that?' I asked. *'Ça, Madame, c'est du Pizza Provençal,'* was the surprising reply. Odd how that Neapolitan pizza has captured people's imaginations, even in Provence, where they have their own traditional version of it, the great difference being that the Provençal variety is made without the top dressing of chewy cheese characteristic of the Neapolitan pizza.

For the dough: *3 tablespoons butter, a generous cup of all-purpose flour, salt, 1 egg, 1 packed tablespoon fresh yeast, a little warm water.* Note: *If you use active dry yeast, use 1½ teaspoons.*

For the filling: *olive oil, 1¼lb (2 large) onions, 2 tomatoes, pepper, salt, about two dozen anchovy fillets, about two dozen small, pitted black olives.*

Cut the butter in little pieces and rub it into the flour. Add a good pinch of salt. Make a well in the center; put in the egg and the yeast dissolved in about 2 tablespoons of warm water. Mix and knead for 5 minutes until the dough comes away clean from the sides of the bowl. Shape into a ball, make a deep cross-cut on the top, put on a floured plate, cover with a floured cloth and leave in a warm place to rise for 2 hours.

Heat 3 or 4 tablespoons of olive oil in a heavy frying pan. Put in the thinly sliced onions and cook them very gently, with the cover on the pan, until they are quite soft and pale golden. They must not fry or turn brown. Add the skinned tomatoes and the seasonings (plus garlic if you like). Continue cooking until tomatoes and onions are amalgamated, and the water from the tomatoes evaporated.

When the dough has risen, sprinkle it with flour and punch it down again. Knead once more into a ball, which you place in the center of an oiled 8-inch tart pan. With your knuckles press it gently but quickly outwards until it is spread right over the pan and all round the sides. Put in the filling. Make a criss-cross pattern all over the top with the anchovies, then fill in with the olives. Leave to rise another 15 minutes. Bake in the center of a preheated oven, with the pan standing on a baking sheet, at 400°F, for 20 minutes, then turn down to 350°F, and bake another 20 minutes.

Enough for four people as a first course.

BOOKS *by* ELIZABETH DAVID

A Book of Mediterranean Food
First published by John Lehmann 1950.

French Country Cooking
First published by John Lehmann 1951.

Italian Food
First published by Macdonald and Co 1954.

Summer Cooking
First published by Museum Press 1955.

French Provincial Cooking
First published by Michael Joseph Ltd 1960.

Spices, Salt and Aromatics in the English Kitchen
First published by Penguin Books 1970.

English Bread and Yeast Cookery
First published by Allen Lane 1977.

An Omelette and a Glass of Wine
First published by Jill Norman at Robert Hale Ltd 1984.

Harvest of the Cold Months
First published by Michael Joseph Ltd 1994.

Elizabeth David's Christmas
First published by Michael Joseph Ltd 2003.

INDEX